A LIFE TOLD IN CATS

CLAIRE ENTWISTLE

A Life Told In Cats

Claire Entwistle

For Mia

A Life Told In Cats

THE WHY OF CATS

'You could buy another one,' said the taxi driver. 'Cheaper, much cheaper than all this. I have heard you can get them for nothing.'

The road was bumpy and the car's suspension less than perfect. I hefted the basket on to my lap to level it out, and also to provide a feeling of closeness. I'm here, I told her silently. She murmured and pressed her face against the bars, and I rubbed her poor cheek with a careful finger. She was panting, must be feeling sick, or terrified, or both.

'That's true, people give them away sometimes,' I said, but it didn't stop him.

'In my country, people cannot afford what you are doing'.

I did not know which country was his or what it had cost him, or perhaps his parents or grandparents, to arrange for our paths to cross in South London this dark February morning.

'No,' I said. I felt awful. The stop-and-start along Walworth Road was making me nauseous, and the conversation was making me wince for the difference in our circumstances, that I should have this luxury of funding a vet's fees and a taxi while he – while he what? I knew nothing about the guy's circumstances or history, only that in this matter we were on completely different wavelengths. If I tried to explain how much the quivering contents of this basket meant to me, could he possibly understand?

But most of all I felt sick with anxiety for my cat, a fizzy cocktail of dread and hope which drowned more subtle thought. We needed to get to the vet in time for the appointment, because it was just possible, though frankly unlikely, that some not too intrusive treatment would help her. But we mustn't arrive too early, because the waiting room would be full of snuffling dogs and noises-off from the treatment rooms which might, by increasing her stress, make her feel even worse. And it was my job to decide what happened next, and how and when to make it happen, whatever 'it' was.

*

I can imagine the man's even more uncomprehending frown if he guessed that years later I would be taking time off from paid employment to write a memoir about the cats in my life. I'm doing it because cats are central to that life, and have been since I was a small child, kneeling on the hall floor waiting for Katy to creep out of my sister's school bag. The driver clearly had other priorities, but I'm not the only person to feel this way. The love our cats receive and offer, the lessons they teach, the huge things they represent, these fragile beings who can be carried around in a basket, so huge and so tiny, gone in a moment and with us forever.

Some people have the good fortune to keep a partner or friends for their whole life, but cats are cyclical, coming and going, coming and going in a rhythm of their own. I am a different person at each stage of the cycle, and a different person again with each cat, or cats. And the Cycle of Cats seems to occur outside of my personal choice, as though it is my unconscious mind or fate deciding what comes next. And that is fascinating.

Fascinating to me, anyway, and perhaps to readers whose own lives might be told in cats. If I could find that taxi driver again, I would like to ask him about his life, ready to listen and attempt to empathise even where my understanding failed. Then I would give him a copy of my book and say, Please, read this kindly – it's my life.

A Life Told In Cats

FOLLOWING A MOON SHADOW: MIA AND POPPY

At the time of writing, I have exchanged South London for Morecambe Bay, the occupant of that long-ago basket has wandered deep into the forest of my memory, and my life contains three flesh-and-blood cats: Poppy, Luna and Charles. And there's Mia, Shadow Cat, who died earlier this year. I'm at that stage in the Cycle of Cats where the shadow is strong, sharper at times than the forms of the living.

So, Mia first. She was a British Shorthair, a pedigree Blue with apricot lights, all smoke and cream and muscle; loose and rounded, orange-eyed, curious, intelligent, patient. Such patience she had. Beside a door she wanted open, or a bowl she wished filled, she would sit, curl her tail around her sturdy paws, and wait, her eyes on whatever or whoever would effect the change.

A most typical British Shorthair was Mia, in nature as well as appearance. Calm, affectionate, the mistress of the deepest relaxation I have ever experienced. And I did experience it. She loved to sit on my knee, take a moment resting her cheek against the back of my hand, then settle with her tail at my waist and extend her body down my legs (I bought a footstool for our favourite chair to accommodate her stretchiness), and rest her head on my feet, then relax deeper and deeper until I relaxed too. My Mia. How I hate to type 'was' and 'used to' into sentences that speak of you, but this is the truth, and has been, now, for long long months. Time continues to pass, and heals, in its way.

Mia: mine, and she was. Names are so important for cats, so full of meaning, so driving of their destiny and ours. 'Luna', for instance, with its hint of other worlds and the resonance of its syllables, so that speaking the word seems to call its owner towards you – 'Lu-na'. I first heard of her on Valentine's Day this year, three weeks and three days after Mia left us, and also the day that my husband gave me a moonstone pendant. With that synchronicity more common in real life than fiction, I was learning to sing an Italian lullaby called La Luna Splende when the message pinged through. I closed the piano and squinted at my phone. A message from a Facebook acquaintance I had never met in real life, concerning a female British Shorthair, three years old, who needed a home. Her name was Luna…

It felt meant. Love was in the air that night, the moon was bright, ripe to burst into full glory in the next few days, by which time, if all went well, my tryst with Luna might be complete. If! If it happened at all, and probably, if I was honest, it should not. Far too early to be thinking of another cat, not even a month since Mia's departure.

My Mia. Her name, so perfect for her and for our relationship, was chosen not by me but by a breeder who had brought her into being and kept her close for six years, producing litter after litter of kittens for sale. It would not have been my choice, but it grew on me, and begat more ethereal forms of address. 'My cloud,' I would murmur as she drifted by, soft and gleaming, 'my silver cloud across the moon.'

The moon! Luna! So you see how when I saw that name, that arrangement of pixels on an iPhone screen, it seemed meant. I took a breath and read the message again. Luna – oh, and her brother Charles – were in temporary accommodation, needing to move soon. Were we interested in taking one or both of them?

In the Cycle of Cats, shadow cats cast shadows of their own. Suddenly it was eight years ago and I was mourning another loss, blundering in the dark, searching, searching for – for Mia, I feel like saying, though I only knew I was looking for a British Blue. A new beginning, a new kind of cat. If in matters of human love we have types, my feline type has been the British Blue from the moment I glimpsed my first one in – of all prosaic places – a cat food advert. Their enchanting appearance could not be doubted, and extensive reading plus a few meetings confirmed their calm and lovely natures. We were looking for a British Blue; an adult, not a kitten, because we'd have felt uneasy spending money on a brand new pedigree when so many older moggies were in need. Really? Sounds like one of those uneasy compromises one makes with one's own principles.

Eight years ago we still lived in London, and Steve and I both still worked full time, and our move to Cumbria and COVID and the Ukraine/Russian war had not been thought of. A straightforward time it seems now, relatively, and the search for Mia – for a British Blue - remains clear in my mind: the googling and the phone calls and the texts which eventually led to a professional breeder in Orpington, a woman called Jan. 'Jan'. Another tiny name, a few pixels on a Nokia screen that changed my life.

Steve and I were used to basic moggies, and entering the pedigree world for the first time, there was lingo to learn. Jan explained that she would soon be 'retiring' – what a terrific word – two 'queens' and a 'stud' from her 'stock', and we were welcome to come and see them. 'Mia is our dominant queen' she added with an air of congratulation, as though setting up a meeting with a celebrity. It was made clear that the audience implied no commitment on either side. Perhaps Jan was suspicious of our motives, as indeed we were of hers - not that she didn't sound above board on the phone, responsible and fond of the cats in her care, but my recent research into kitten and puppy breeding had thrown up a few horror stories. I was imagining something like a farm, and only hoped the conditions were good.

In fact, it was nothing like a farm. We drew up outside a modest bungalow on a slip road and were taken into the conservatory which opened into a paved garden dotted with little prefab buildings. Jan pointed out the separate 'lodges' for 'boys' and 'girls', and the individual pens for those who were nursing kittens. It all looked neat and clean. Radio 3 was playing 24/7 from a transistor radio on a hook on the fence. 'It soothes their nerves,' she said. I wondered how soothed the neighbours were, with non-stop sonatas and highbrow talks blaring over the fence.

Recalling those grim accounts of overcrowding, it was cheering to discover that the cats were allowed in the garden during the day – girls and boys separately, like a Victorian school treat – and into the very conservatory in which we were standing. The sound of unfamiliar voices soon had the space rippling with feline curiosity, and there, springing atop the table and stepping forward to greet us, came Mia, Dominant Queen. Retiring? Mia looked a lot fitter than Steve and me, but Jan explained she was six years old and recovering from 'a difficult kittening' which meant she'd needed a hysterectomy.

What a beauty, centre stage on the polished wood table, blue-grey silk shot with cream, chunky circles for eyes and face, body and tail, that intent expression and calm demeanour so typical of British Shorthairs. Just looking at her calmed me even as it lifted my spirits. Yes, please! Steve was smiling too, and our new friend accepted a stroke from each of us. Mia: Mine. She wasn't yet, but she would be.

'You might as well meet the other two,' said Jan, correctly reading our reaction, and led us down the garden path to the Girls' quarters. A forest of cat trees and litter trays blossomed with feline beauties, any or all of which I would gladly have swept into the car and driven home. Most of them looked up with a friendly blink and several moved forward for a stroke; human attention must have been in short supply. But they were working girls, Jan cautioned, and unavailable.

'But you can have Alfie,' she said, pointing to the sturdiest cat tree which overflowed with grey and white fluff in a shape recalling Winston Churchill's later years. Alfie was soft and handsome, his expression benign and wise, but he looked over-fed and absolutely exhausted, not even moving to greet us, though he managed an amiable grunt.

'*Should* he be in with the girls?'

'Yes, he's neutered now, wouldn't get on with the boys'.

We didn't enquire what led to his retirement, but I could not help thinking of the phrase 'shagged out'. He wasn't what we were looking for, and I silently wished him luck finding a home.

'And there's Poppy. She's a Scottish Fold. There, down there.'

On the bottom shelf of the lowest tree stood the smallest member of the Girls' lodge, her torti-white colouring, once you knew where to look, standing out amongst the greys and blues. She had the tiny, folded-back ears of her breed, which Jan explained started with a mutation in a Scottish farm cat, and nowadays combined with Shorthair genes to create Poppy and her ilk. The strange little ears and dark lines which surrounded her eyes like kohl combined to create a permanently astonished expression which was quite charming.

I stretched out a hand, and Poppy jumped back.

'Go on,' said Jan.

'Really?' I had learnt only to approach a cat who was willing.

'Go on.'

My hand reached out again and followed Poppy's retreating head, counter-intuitively rubbing it whenever possible until her dismay abruptly changed to bliss and she lay on her back, purring for more.

'She's a sweet cat, but nervous,' said Jan. 'If you want to take her, it will have to be with Alfie or Mia. She wouldn't know what to do on her own.'

Wouldn't know what to do? I had never heard of such a thing. Cats always knew what to do.

Anyway, we only wanted one cat, had already chosen Mia, but I lingered over Poppy.

'Did she need a hysterectomy too?'

'No, she's always been healthy, but she won't mate any more. She lies on her side and refuses to cooperate, whatever the stud does to persuade her'.

Alfie grunted again, and I wondered if this strenuous and perhaps humiliating experience had contributed to his current state.

'Anyway, you can take Mia or Alfie on their own, or Poppy with either of the others, or all three of them of course, if you have the space. Most Shorthairs like a bit of cat company, though it's not essential'.

It was a mild injunction, but enough to ensure that when we returned a week later to collect Mia, having dutifully spent some time weighing up the decision we had made in the first five seconds, Poppy tagged along. Perhaps we had already decided to become a two-cat household, but without realising it. The Cycle of Cats was moving on.

It was always Mia and Poppy, never Poppy and Mia. Mia, whose entourage of twenty-two pedigree underlings had abruptly reduced to one small, bemused subject with flat ears, set the pace for their settling-in period. She led Poppy under the sofa for the statutory hiding stage, then out again (in record time) to explore the room, then the rest of the house, and later the garden. I began to see what Jan meant by Poppy not knowing what to do on her own. She was always looking around for Mia, eating when she ate, ideally from the same bowl, or attempting to join any game Mia was engaged in, even when there was only one feather-on-a-stick and a single human hand to wield it. If Mia sat looking out of a window, there Poppy would be, behind or beside her, peering over her shoulder. When Mia settled down for a rest, Poppy would recognise her chosen spot as the most desirable and attempt to simultaneously occupy it herself, receiving a swat from a heavy grey paw. Mia made no attempt to hide her irritation, but the two of them would eventually settle down, curled up a few inches apart but in the same position, facing the same way like sheep in a field.

Clearly Mia was in every way the more powerful of the two and I wondered about bullying, but their needs turned out to be deeply compatible. In human terms, Mia was the retired company director hoping to channel his energies into reorganising the local Neighbourhood Watch group, Poppy the bewildered householder who was only too thankful that somebody appeared to know what they were doing.

Mia's needs and mine were also compatible. I had heard that British Shorthairs prefer to sit near to their human friends but not touching, so it was a joyful surprise when she climbed on to my lap and melted into a level of relaxation I had failed to achieve through decades of yoga and meditation. As ever, Poppy attempted to follow her although Mia made it clear with growls and shoves that there was only room for one on my lap, and that the Mine in Mia went both ways: I belonged to her now. The two of us grew closer and closer, starting the morning with a delicate kiss on the nose and pausing many times a day to hold each other's gaze or simply watch each other. I loved to rest my eyes on the moving spheres of her face and body, the thoughtful expression of her tilted head, the deep calm of her heavy limbs. I can't tell what she saw in me, but it was something that made her eyes glow even brighter and her soft face softer still.

All this mutual adoration must have been hard for Poppy to witness. For eight years she strove to get as close to me as her mentor, thrusting her bright head between Mia's cheek and my stroking fingers. Steve and I took care to pay her attention too, whereupon Poppy would creep just out of reach and stare imploringly. We would stretch to stroke her, then shuffle forwards as she retreated again, repeating the process until we got cramp and had to give up. Now I wonder whether, back in her time at the breeder's, she had been hoping the stud would take the same 'no means yes' view of her reluctance to join in.

For Poppy's own safety I could only show affection when Mia was out of the room, so Steve offered to take on the position of her best friend, but their relationship had none of the effortless grace of mine with Mia. Poppy would only let him stroke her properly on the middle shelf of her special cat tree. She would fetch him for this purpose from his second-floor studio several times a day, standing in the doorway with her mouth stretched in a silent meow, urgent eyes a-glow, until he sighed and followed her down to the cat tree, where she would proceed to arrange herself in a sequence of postures, like a pole dancer: upright with upright tail, head down and bottom in the air, hugging the scratching post with both arms, lying on her left side then her right. Steve would dutifully stroke each area as it was presented to him, until she indicated it was time to stop by scratching her left ear with her back foot, scrambling into the top level of the tree and falling deeply asleep. Mia, observing this charade from the kitchen table, would follow the process with her patient gaze, occasionally glancing at me to see what I made of it. Can cats roll their eyes?

Always Mia and Poppy; never Poppy and Mia. We soon discovered that Mia was ill, some chronic systemic thing whose symptoms came and went, failing to show up in the tests which were so traumatic for Mia that she became less trusting not just of vets but of strangers in general and, when she was most unwell, downright unfriendly to any visitors who dared to show up at the house, acquiring a reputation for ill-temper which I thought was unfair. Nobody is at their best when everything hurts… She had long periods of good health and spirits, thank God, especially in the early years, but they were increasingly interspersed with spells of lassitude, yelping as though in pain, and a worrying refusal some days to eat or drink. The vet agreed that it would be unkind to keep repeating investigations which had never showed anything useful, and offered painkillers instead.

Being so close to her, I felt her discomfort quite physically at times, the stress of it, and I rejoiced in the way it would drain away into my lap when we settled together on our chair, my feet up on the footstool and her chin on my ankle, her body thinner and rougher-haired as years went by and the illness progressed, but always beautiful and always able, right to the end, to relax and soften, to lay her head against my wrist and smile up at me with her amber eyes. She was my relaxation, my peace; my sadness too, in those last months, as the sands of her life ran out.

A Life Told In Cats

THE CAT IS DEAD: LONG LIVE THE CAT.

My sweet momento mori. I remember as a child, a neighbour – ancient to me, probably about 70 – saying that he would not get another cat after Tibbles in case he died while the cat was still alive. I was shocked that he would compare lifespans so coolly, and his words stayed with me. We all know that unless you are as old as Cyril next door felt at the time, or seriously ill, you are likely to outlive any cat who enters the flap of your heart. You meet your new friend and know, if you allow yourself to know it, that one day you'll be mourning her loss. Painful, yet we keep doing it.

So, we lost Mia in January this year, and while her presence remained in the house for an uncanny few weeks, as often happens when a pet dies, our thoughts turned in a new way to Poppy. The cat is dead; long live the cat. Life must go on and a home needs a cat, but was Poppy up to the challenge of being Sole, and therefore in effect Chief Cat? We feared that, accustomed to copying Mia whatever she did, Poppy might simply follow her into the Light. There was no moment when we saw the little orange sidekick recognise that her leader was gone, but she seemed out of sorts, sleeping the day away in solitude, eating less, rarely coming to ask Steve for a stroke. This pattern had formed a while before Mia died, but Steve and I had both been focused on Mia, in our different ways, and paid little attention.

Perhaps Poppy had understood better than anyone how close the end was. Now we began to worry. Mia had not been especially nice to Poppy, but she had been absolutely central to the way she lived.

A fortnight after she died I paced the Mia-less house, acknowledging each spot where she especially loved to sit – oh, the basket in the kitchen, lined with my best fleecy jumper, which was almost part of her towards the end, and the bathroom where she greeted me every morning, ready to play with tap water - and tried to focus on Poppy, whom I hadn't seen for hours. Poppy, all on her own. Should we find her a companion, and if so what manner of cat; another Blue or something different? Here she was, snoring on a spare bed in an empty study, flat on her side, paws stacked in front of her. She didn't look comfortable and she didn't open her eyes when approached. I loved her, her well-kempt fur and tiny ears, her sweet eccentricity, but living with her in her fourteenth year was not really like living with a cat at all. She only appeared a couple of times a day to accept, if encouraged, a quick stroke on level two of the cat tree before setting off back upstairs for another twelve hours. And she slept so deeply; surely she should have woken when I came close. Perhaps she needed another cat in her life, someone to look up to and compete with. Like Steve and me, perhaps she missed the presence of a fully functioning cat, a working model that did proper cat things.

Mia was irreplaceable, of course, of course, but on the other hand British Blues have so much in common... Sighing over photos on the internet ('kitty porn', they call this on the social media sites) I saw over and over again Mia's head tilt, her thoughtful gaze, her solid curves. But she wouldn't *be* Mia, I reminded myself, she might behave differently in some crucial way, such as ignoring me, perhaps, in favour of Steve. Still, I'd be able to admire her beautiful appearance, if only from a distance... A kitten maybe, this time? The prices were alarming, but even worse was the thought of a kitten's vulnerability. I don't like to keep cats indoors unless they prefer it or are ill, and shuddered at the prospect of watching a mini-Mia set off outside for the first time, exuberant and untaught. Poppy, however well disposed, could not be relied upon to offer traffic awareness training; she was more likely to follow a familiar blue shape into the road. Not a kitten; I lacked the emotional stamina and, anyway, doubted that Poppy could stand anything so lively after all her years with such a dignified, and lately sick, companion.

So, a calm and wise adult, preferably used to going outside, but not an elderly one, dear God no, grant us we beseech thee a good few years of health and spirits. An adult Shorthair, if one was available, but not from a breeder this time, because why would a breeder let go a youngish animal in perfect health? Whatever led to Mia's last pregnancy going so wrong was likely connected to the illness that gradually killed her.

Not a kitten, not a retired queen. It was sounding like a rescue cat then; the cherished companion of someone needing residential care, or perhaps an impulse buy from the 2020 lockdown, fully grown, less 'cute' than when she was tiny and far more expensive to run, with the cost of living crisis. Surely with a bit of persistence we could find one? If not from a rescue place, then from a private person? The first cat I sourced myself came from an advert in the public library. Even if we couldn't find a Shorthair, perhaps there would another type of cat with a similar temperament who Poppy would recognise as one of her tribe.

But there was nothing. Back in the day it was an easy matter; you just left the cat flap open and came downstairs one morning to find your new friend washing her face on your kitchen table, or you mentioned that you were looking and were beset by desperate owners seeking a good home for a pet they could no longer care for. Not any more, it seemed; not in 2022, even if you were unfussy about the breed. Local shelters advertised a tiny selection, and there was always some reason why we failed to meet their spec, or vice versa – the cats came as a bonded pair, which sounded like bad news for Poppy, and/or were indoor-only, which wouldn't work with Poppy used to an open cat flap policy, and/or they couldn't live with other animals. Or the cats were all marked 'reserved' but were still on the website when you looked a couple of weeks later. What was going on there?

I was aware that much of this mental and keyboard activity was a displacement activity intended to the fill the hours until Mia's demise should take its place in my psyche as a dark but inevitable phase in the great Cycle of Cats. I was aware that my cunning plan to increase Poppy's comfort by bringing in reinforcements was based on little more than wishful thinking. I also suspected that if the tide of my unconscious was surging in the direction of another two-cat household, there was little I could do to stop it.

So I decided to put a message on a Facebook group I belong to: 'Archers Cats'. I don't know why fans of the Radio 4 'contemporary drama in a rural setting' exhibit a higher than average enthusiasm for domestic moggies, but it seems to be the case, and the group is popular. Its members are generous with advice both professional and homespun, eager to share and enjoy each others' photos and stories, supportive in times of trouble. When I posted news of Mia's death, dozens of responses appeared within minutes, all of them sympathetic. Pretty impressive, when you think how nasty social media sites can quickly turn.

'Anyone know of a British Shorthair female, two to five years old, able to live with an older cat, used to going outdoors, located in striking distance of Cumbria?' I paused, read my post back and added, 'I know it's a long shot.' Nobody disagreed with that last comment, but as usual the group's response was kind and constructive. Several members replied sending good wishes and suggesting rescue places I already knew of; nothing immediately useful, but I had a feeling that some would remember my request and get back to me if they heard of anything.

Meanwhile, I evoked the services of Google, was directed to private adverts, and entered a pet-trading underworld I had never known existed. There were plenty of adverts for Shorthairs, but so dodgy! Un-spayed females allegedly living in a barn with access to the outside, yet mysteriously un-bothered by the tom cats on surrounding farms, price £400. Terse messages that 'I need to sell my 8-year-old tabby because I'm too busy to look after him, £500, no time-wasters'. How could they? It must have been a side effect of COVID which made pets so suddenly desirable to stay-at-home individuals and families, madly inflating the prices.

It was all very disheartening, but the temptation was great, and I got as far as a phone call with a local woman advertising a stunning two-year-old female Shorthair, jet black with brilliant blue eyes. The advertiser insisted that she was 'not a breeder', claiming instead that, ordinary cat lover as she was, she had happened to own an entire tom at the same time as an un-spayed queen, and the two of them produced one litter of kittens she'd hoped to keep, but now she was being evicted from her rented flat and had to let them go. What? She was renting a flat but had enough money to buy two active pedigrees which would have retailed at thousands?? I felt like suggesting that in future she save her money for a deposit on a property of her own, but of course I didn't. My enquiry as to why, on the vaccination certificate she texted over, the owner's name and address were heavily crossed out, only led to accusations of time-wasting and an end to our correspondence. It was sad; the cat was beautiful, her future uncertain and her dodgy origins not her fault, but she might have been stolen, or perhaps been bred by an amateur without precautions against inherited disease. I didn't want to encourage a trade in stolen animals, and couldn't face taking on another ailing creature straight after Mia.

Then, just as I was resigning myself to spending extra time with Poppy in the hope of cheering her up and satisfying my own needs for a cat in my life, Archers Cats came good. A fellow Shorthair devotee, remembering my post, put me in touch with the breeder who had provided her own two gorgeous, jet-black Shorthair brothers whose photos had often made me smile. Karen, the breeder was called, and it was she who sent me that fateful Facebook message on Valentine's Day.

We were in business. I expressed interest and Karen offered more details. No talk of time wasting on either side; we all wanted the cats to be happily settled with happy humans. Karen explained that she had sold this sibling pair as kittens three years ago, but they were about to become homeless because the couple who bought them had separated, and neither was able to keep the cats. The parents of one of the original owners had taken them in short-term, and were showing signs of strain since it became clear that neither of the young people had plans to take them back.

Two healthy pedigrees, no charge. They wouldn't be available for long, not in this strange climate. The cats were currently living in Okehampton, a long way from Cumbria, but surely it would be worth the inconvenience of going to collect them. Even though my motion sickness and Steve's back problem make long distance driving difficult. Even though two cat carriers on the train would be a nightmare...

But the name - Luna! Valentine's Day, the moonstone, silver light over Morecambe Bay beyond our window, the lilting magic of La Luna Splende. Luna felt like fate. There was Charles too, the brother, but he didn't feel like fate at all and, rereading Karen's message, I hoped it would be OK to ask for just his sister. I've always had females, and anyway Steve and I were adamant that we couldn't take on two cats, leaving poor Poppy outnumbered by strangers. The plan would only work if Charles found a home elsewhere. All those concerned were Shorthairs, guaranteed calm and friendly. Poppy and Luna would soon settle together, and Charles elsewhere. Luna! My Cloud across the moon; Mia's consecrated successor.

I suggested this to Karen, who did not actually say no and sent a few photos of the cats provided by their reluctant owners, rather poor ones given that they were in effect publicity shots. In the first photo Charles was being held up in the air by somebody just out of shot, and the proportions looked rather strange, his head tiny and his body lopsided. The second showed Luna, face-on and bolt upright, glaring at the camera. The final picture was Charles again, crouched on the ground and squinting.

Why was there no picture of the siblings together? Did they actually get on? Karen's message suggested that although she wasn't ruling out our offer to take just Luna, she'd only separate the two as a last resort. They had already faced a lot of disruption; the one constant was being together, and they might pine on their own. Then there was another problem which we guessed at, though Karen did not mention it: if Luna was homed on her own, Charles might not be so easy to place because he'd lost an eye at birth due to an infection. Closer examination of his photo showed that he had one eyelid sewn up, giving him a comical appearance of using a monocle, and the visible eye was not huge and golden, but smallish and pale, and in general he looked rather slight for a male, lacking the heavy jowls and broad shoulders that were so remarkable in Alfie. We didn't mind, but some potential owners wanting a pedigree might be more inclined to take Charles alongside his golden-eyed sister. Luna! She was indeed somewhat but not too much like Mia; not 'blue' but a dark silver-grey with tabby markings, sturdy but less rounded, taller and more stately. La luna splende.

Steve, when consulted, was also concerned about Charles's prospects. It never occurred to us to offer to home the brother on his own; we had a female in mind (not that we were trying to replace Mia, of course) and then there was the name. Luna... The next thing was that we had talked ourselves into believing that two new cats would be fine; no harder for Poppy to adjust to than one, and they would find it easier to settle together, which would make the whole process even smoother. Oh, the treachery of a thought process, presenting itself as logical, that has already reached its conclusion. We wanted Luna, so we went for her.

The whole situation echoed the Orpington episode of eight years ago, in which our decision to take home a single cat mysteriously yielded a pair. Perhaps we had unknowingly decided to have three cats this time. Perhaps next time it will be four, then five, which will be no easy matter with the rocketing price of cat food. I sometimes feel quite defenceless in the face of my unconscious decisions.

Be that as it may, that is the story of how there come to be three living cats in my life, Poppy, Luna and Charles. I place them in that order because Poppy, first come and served, remains our priority, though the bulk of my cat-thoughts divide between Luna and Mia. Moon and Moon Shadow. I'm still being followed, still following.

*

We were supported in our logical entrechat by two old friends who live close to Okehampton and offered to drive the cats up to Cumbria for us. We were fully aware that it made sense for us to go down and meet the cats before committing. We knew virtually nothing about them except their names and breed. A video would have helped, but there wasn't one, and we didn't want to bother the reluctant hosts more than necessary. But our friends offered to bring them down... and we knew they understood what it entailed and would do a fine job because they had transported Poppy and Mia from London when we first moved north... But the trouble, for them! 'It seems too much to ask', I demurred, and they said 'You didn't ask, we offered'. But they had a lot on, and could only make the journey very soon, the coming weekend in fact, the weekend after Valentine's Day.

Just a couple of days to decide the fate of these two cats, not to mention Steve's and mine. We had family staying, young people of different generations and genders, by nobody's definition 'mad cat ladies', but all in their own way devotees. The subject of the possible new recruits was exhaustively discussed. Yes or no? There was much to say on both sides, and it was dutifully said, though all of us inclined to more cats rather than fewer. Eventually I acknowledged that though I had quite a few reservations (it was too soon; we didn't know what they'd be like; three was too many), and I felt somewhat relieved to imagine just continuing with Poppy for the moment, I wanted to go ahead anyway. Steve felt the same.

I really don't know why we bothered with all that. I'd decided when I read Karen's first message.

And so that Saturday afternoon, a familiar car drew up outside our house bringing two cat baskets, a boot full of equipment and reports of a peaceful journey. No wailing, no fisticuffs, no drama, feline or human, even though the weather was poor, storms threatening, and traffic bad. Classic shorthair good nature all round. In my memory the moon was up, silvering the sands outside the tall windows of our front room, as the two carriers were opened and two cautious shapes emerged; though in fact they arrived in daylight, thanks to our friends stopping only for one quick break, and the moon must have risen hours later. Memory so quickly edits and improves, reorganising events to prove the rememberer right or wrong.

I'm pretty sure that Luna was the first out, the first to accept a head rub and sniff the bowl of biscuits, while Charles lingered in his carrier. Luna's golden gaze and sturdy paws took the measure of the room: along, down, under, up, over. Just as I'd hoped: here was our new Chief Cat. The Queen is dead; long live the Queen. Sorry, Poppy, but it's what you're used to. Luna was taller than Mia, darker and as handsome in her own way. Round golden eyes like Mia's, but not so much curious and open as watchful and anxious. As you'd expect, I assured myself, at the start of this major life change. How could she know what possibilities this house contained for her, what love beat in its heart?

A Life Told In Cats

Charles, slender-legged and about half his sister's size, had creamy fur touched at the nose and ears with chocolate brown which reminded me of Jessica, a family cat from long ago. Jessica: the sealpoint Siamese unthought-of for years, whose shadow now fell with sweet clarity across this new arrival as he crept forward and looked up at me. Charles's sewn-up eyelid gave him the air of squinting that I remembered from the photo, but in real life its disabling effects were more obvious. He was constantly tilting and turning his head, which still seemed a tad small for the body, and he moved more hesitantly than his sister. Lack of binocular vision, of course. I know because I suffer from that too, though my right eye is not, like his, sewn up, but unusable due to neurological damage.

God, I thought, watching Charles's head swivel to assess the space that his sister had processed in a series of swift glances. God, that looks like hard work. Poor old Charles. Bet his neck hurts. Just like mine. I hope people don't look at me and think, Poor old Claire. But I hope they realise that it can be difficult, tiring too, tilting your head to see things. But I hope they don't pity me. But I hope they understand. But I hope they don't pity me... Poor old Charles. But he does very well really. Oh heck, patronising or what. He's a cat, just get to know him.

Charles seemed keen to postpone that process. After the briefest tour of the room he discovered that the curtain over the bay window was long and thick, and managed to wrap himself in the overlap, vanishing for several hours. Luna meanwhile circled the humans, stopping for an occasional greeting, jumping from time to time on to the narrow sill of the smallest, highest window. Jumping, I say — she half-stepped, half-flew up there, as though to her the three dimensions were one. My mind flicked the album of Mia's eight years with me. How she could leap, right from the first day, though she'd had little opportunity at the breeder's to hone her skills. Poppy too, when tempted with a feather on a string; right up into the air, from standing, as though she were a tiddlywink or a flea. In their later years, age and arthritis and sickness had limited the movement of both cats; chairs had to be organised to access favourite spots, upstairs windows closed to prohibit stunts based on Mia's ideas of her younger self. There would be no need for that kind of caution in the new regime. Poppy liked to stay close to the ground and Charles, a motionless bulge in the curtain material, was showing similar tendencies. And Luna could obviously handle herself. A thud, and she was back at my feet, flicking me a glance the clear gold of Mia's. But with, oh, such a different expression. Could this really work?

A Life Told In Cats

EARLY SHADOWS: KATY AND JESSICA

How long will Mia remain Shadow Cat, her memory bleakly contrasting the characters and habits of her successors? Months, I think, rather than years; she is fading a little already, though you never forget a cat you have truly loved, just as you never forget a person or a place. You may think you have forgotten, but you find them fast enough when you look. A shadow which time has faded to sepia but which, when you start to focus, bursts into colour and sound and motion, and the cat is back. Long live the cat.

Is, perhaps, the first cat the deepest? Mine was Katy, short for Catrina, as in 'Cat', you see; my sister and I, who had the naming of her, found the word play brilliantly funny at the time, but we were only eight and five. My parents had had no intention of getting a cat until the day that Daisy arrived home from school announcing that her class teacher was awarding kittens to a few good girls for outstanding work and conduct, and that Daisy was one of the chosen. All lies of course; the teacher obviously had a glut of kittens and was scraping the barrel of potential homes; but Mum fell for it, even Daisy's claim that parents were not allowed to come into school to collect the little furry prizes from the teacher in question, thus allowing the story to be checked out.

So Katy came into our lives, emerging from my sister's school bag small, stripy and cross. Mum gave her time for a tour of the room then taught me how to stroke her. 'Always from the top of the head to the base of the tail, never ruffle the fur, go gently, gently now'. Always gently. I remembered that gentleness. I remembered it twenty-five years later at a workshop in which we were asked 'As a child, who in your life was the centre of warmth?' I wasn't sure at first, then her face appeared: a classic tabby M on a soft forehead, grape-green eyes that stared past you into the more interesting distance. A twitching tail. Katy.

It shocked me a bit to make that discovery, that the cat was my warmest childhood contact, especially since she wasn't, in all honesty, a particularly nice cat. She would hide under the hall table and jump out as you walked past, especially barelegged, and fasten her little claws into your shins. Extremely painful, but Mum said that if it happened, you had to stand there until she let go, because pushing or kicking might hurt her. Cats were fragile, small-boned, sensitive. Unlike the rest of us, was the implication, and her vulnerability made Katy special – safer, somehow, to love fully.

And my mother and sister and I all did love her fully, gladly enduring the scratched limbs and ruined carpets, the supply of rodents, dead and alive, that needed rescuing or burying, and the constant challenges to human authority. She soon developed tactics for getting her own way which weirdly echoed the means by which she arrived in our home. Relegated to the kitchen overnight, Katy would exit the cat flap and come round to my window sill, meowing and tapping the glass until I got up to open the door for her. Confined once more to the kitchen after breakfast, in a bid to preserve the soft furnishings during working hours, she would lurk under the bushes next to the porch, ready to shoot inside and behind some immovable item of furniture as soon as the last person opened the front door to leave the house. Come the evening, she would stake out a favourite chair for hours on end, leaping on to its seat and hissing at whichever occupant had stood up to go to the loo or change the TV channel.

The females of the household united in admiring rather than deploring this behaviour. Even my mother did, though I once caught her examining a torn stocking in the hall and muttering 'You're only the cat, you know'. When the price of Whiskas went up she added, 'I could afford to smoke if not for you'. But those were isolated incidents. The morning started with Mum's happy voice greeting Katy in the kitchen where she waited below the wall-mounted tin opener which was always operated first thing, before the kettle or shower.

My father was less entranced. Unable to resist any species of challenge, he was always trying to outwit her: by leaving the house through the back door of a morning, or making as if to sit on her when she annexed his chair, or kicking and cursing at a fluffy footstool which resembled her in size and colouring, making me shriek with distress while Katy sneered from beneath the sofa. She knew he wouldn't dare.

The centre of warmth in my young life? She could be warm. There was the purring weight of her on my bedspread during the dark hours, after we gave up confining her to the kitchen. There was the dappled beauty of her, coiled on a sunny window seat. There was Mum's cheerful voice in the morning, and the sight of her hand caressing soft fur, head to tail as she'd taught me, evoking the warm putter of Katy's purr. Warmth. The centre of warmth. The one who was always loved, who brought out gentleness in the others. Except Dad, of course.

Katy was also the first cat I lost, many years later, when I was living away from home. She progressed from sixteen years of rude health to vomiting, neatly, into vases on windowsills, then kidney failure. Mum had her put to sleep during my final year at University, during Autumn term, and stoically reported back on the phone as though it was just one of those things: 'it was very peaceful, darling, she went to sleep as I stroked her, and she looked so pretty…' There was no drama; she just wasn't there when I came home for the holidays. But Mum seemed sadder than she had sounded on the phone.

'I'm not enjoying Christmas as much as I expected,' she mused, stirring the rum sauce for the pudding. 'I thought it might be because this is the first one without my mother (Gran had died in November), but I think it's because Katy isn't here.'

Some speculate that people who form strong attachments to their pets are using them as child-substitutes. It's an interesting question. I would not call my cats 'babies' or refer to myself as 'mummy', because I like to honour their separateness and also the fact that they are adults of their own species who need a degree of autonomy rightly denied human children. Choosing to hang out on the roof at 3am, for example, or drinking from puddles. Does it make a difference if someone has their own children? Mothers who are also 'mummy' to their pets no doubt have the distinction clear in their minds, and would always prioritise their children over their cat. Wouldn't you, Mum? If the house was burning down, maybe?

'Of course,' says the shadow mother in my heart, but I point to the scratched young shins beside the hall table, and her mouth twitches.

'If it was something really important, darling, of course you would come first. But cats have feelings too.'

Indeed they do; and cats are also inordinately easy to love, for those of us who are that way inclined. Easier than people? In some ways. People come and go, they have to, they have things to do in the outside world, whereas a cat is part of the fabric of the home. I love my cats in the way I love my home, which is a lot, the bricks and mortar and the views from its windows as well as the living creatures within. I love people too, but they are so much more complicated, the possibilities for hurt and misunderstanding and betrayal so much greater. Which do I love more? The question makes no sense.

Perhaps Mum felt the same way. She was pleased that I was enjoying myself at University, would have been deeply troubled if I was in trouble, but Katy was with her every day. She ventured no further than the fence, reporting for duty beneath the tin opener at breakfast and on one of the beds at night; between times playing her games and pursuing her feuds and resting in various beautiful positions, and occasionally rewarding us with displays of affection: rolling, meowing, exposing a tummy for a stroke and then fastening her claws around the hand that reached out...

A Life Told In Cats

Maybe it is simply that they stay in the home whereas we humans don't. I went away to University and, beguiled by new experience, relaxed my connection with home and cat to the extent that I barely mourned Katy's loss; at least until that moment a quarter of a century later when some ill-advised facilitator carelessly asked 'so who was the centre of warmth in your early years?'.

A cat-less home can be a terrible thing. A cat in the house is the beating heart in the body; the body continues a while without it, but soon becomes something terribly different. But Katy did not leave the house catless, which is perhaps why I missed her less than might have been expected, returning home at the end of that term. Jessica remained.

Jessica had been introduced by my father around the time Katy turned fifteen. I don't remember my opinion being sought on the question of whether to get a second cat; probably not, as I only lived at home during the holidays. I'm not certain that my mother was consulted either, but then she had given Katy the green light on her own initiative, so it was tit for tat.

Dad was more upfront about Jessica's provenance than Daisy had been about Katy's, but there was a back-story, Jessica having been 'made', as Dad put it, by some business friends he needed to impress, who had recently set up a Siamese breeding enterprise on a farm in Wales. Jessica arrived a pure white kitten with tiny chocolate points, an exuberant pouncing creature with none of Katy's sourness, and perhaps because Dad drove to collect her from Wales and served her first meal, Jessica adored him from the start, and her feelings were returned. There was no competition for chairs of an evening, no assault on cat-coloured items of furniture; she sat on Dad's knee or on the footstool beside him. My Snowflake, Dad called her when she was tiny, and was sad when her coat darkened with age. My Snowflake.

So there was an era with two cats in the household, furious Katy spitting at a gleaming imp who teased and outshone her, batting ping pong balls into Katy's path as she mooched by, streaking up a curtain and dancing on the picture rail while human hands stretched up in anxious admiration and, on a window sill far below, her ageing rival growled and threw up into another vase.

The two cats, new and old, grew to tolerate each other, but were never friends, and Mum felt bad for allowing Jessica to complicate Katy's final year. When I look back at this time, my memory offers snapshots rather than a video. Opening the sitting-room door to find Mum seated in her chair by the gas fire and Jessica on the hearthrug purring into the flames, and Mum saying, 'I brought her in to sit on my knee, but she prefers talking to the fire...' She looked wounded. Or again: Mum in her chair, the fire on, Katy in her usual place in the centre of Mum's lap and Jessica squashed between Mum's arm and the arm of the chair. That was where I used to sit for stories when I was little... And Mum looked happier.

Dad looked happier too, whistling for his Snowflake and throwing her up in the air as he had his own babies. I hated it and used to scream, apparently, but like the infant Daisy, Jessica enjoyed a bit of rough and tumble. She and Dad rarely fell out, and when they did, it was only over Jessica taking the opportunity to have a good wash while she was sitting with him. He was affronted, disgusted even, that she should take such liberties on his knee.

Jessica did not seem to mind these occasional fallings-out, which were completely one sided. She adored attention of any kind, even someone plonking her on the floor and telling her off. She loved to be spoken to and would reply in a yowl considerably louder than was needed. When we four humans had some matter to discuss between ourselves, she would sit in the centre of the circle and howl until we fixed our eyes on her, adding the word 'Jessica' to every other sentence.

'Order! Address your remarks through the Cat', someone would say, and we'd laugh, then pay Jessica some compliment before she could take further offence.

'We four humans', I said there. If Katy had divided the family three-one, Jessica made us a foursome.

But it was upsetting for Katy, this rival in her home, and my own memory of this time, though consciously forgotten decades earlier, probably made me less inclined to get a kitten while Poppy was still with us. We could not have some bouncy little upstart taking the mick out of our Poppy, sweet nervous Poppy who had always lived in the shadow of her clever grey companion. Shadow cat! Poppy isn't Katy. I can hardly imagine two beings more unalike, but the old feelings return, applying themselves willy-nilly to some new situation, and before you know what's happened, your unconscious has steered you in some bizarre direction you never planned. Like offering a home to two cats instead of

one, for example, two unknown quantities,   unseen,
all the way down in Okehampton.

A Life Told In Cats

EXTRAS

Maybe Mum's unconscious mind also took the lead when it came to acquiring cats. She accepted Daisy's yarn about pets being given as prizes with a suspicious lack of suspicion. The mother I knew would have intuited the truth: that the teacher in question had offered surplus kittens to her class, hoping that the requisite number of pupils would pressurise their parents into taking one. Maybe it was time for a new cat in Mum's life, but she only realised when one appeared. Maybe, years later, she acquiesced with similar mildness to Jessica's arrival because she anticipated Katy's demise and could not bear it to coincide with her children flying the nest.

'I couldn't live without a cat,' she told me seriously a long time later. Perhaps during my childhood she was in denial about this gap in her life, or perhaps she hoped that her children would fill it. However it came about, she made Katy central to her household, and installed a replacement before Katy even left. I imagine this is how Katy saw it, anyway, however much Dad enthused about the charm of Siamese kittens and the need to support his business friends. Then Jessica became central too. Two aspiring Chief Cats under one roof: a recipe for discomfort.

Other cats arrived in the family home after Katy departed, but they remained peripheral, like extras on the stage of a drama. The first two were

Daisy's. She'd got married and had a baby, and her cats took exception to the noise and the diversion of attention, registering their concerns in a series of 'memos' whose lingering smells were impossible to remove from the carpet. Transported to the family home, they instantly settled in, so relieved to be somewhere quiet that they overlooked Jessica's attention-grabbing and lead clean, unobtrusive lives while she retained centre stage. I surmise that there is always a Chief Cat, and things go well if everyone agrees who it is.

A year or two later I added to the company. I was living in London by then, and one of my flatmates came across a stray kitten hanging around the hospital where she worked, and swept her up and brought her back, without consultation, to our smallish, gardenless flat on a main road. A box of dry food and a litter tray appeared in the kitchen, purchased from our food kitty, it transpired, which irritated the other two flatmates, though I liked the idea of a feline being financed from a 'kitty' too much to complain.

I probably benefited the most from the company of Caz, short for Casualty. It was at the foot of my bed that she purred the night away. When it transpired that her soi-disant owner was planning to leave her alone in the flat for Christmas week, I popped Caz into my holdall and took her home on the train. She lay so quietly on top of my clothes that I was able to open the zip a little way to give her air, and the man in the seat opposite jumped when he caught sight of her gleaming, curious eyes.

When we reached home, Caz assessed the situation and, like Daisy's cats before her, determined to be no trouble. Her modest demeanour, her hanging back from the food bowls, suited the other residents, and though I took her back to London with me after Christmas, Caz made the return trip at Easter and stayed on for the rest of her life, being no trouble.

I've heard that this accommodating behaviour is fairly typical of cats who have been fending for themselves outdoors, or have lived with people less than committed to taking care of them, provided there has been no major trauma. What surprises me now is that *Mum* was so accommodating. Our downstairs flat and garden were huge; no shortage of space, but there was all the expense and trouble, not to mention the wear and tear on the furniture. She was not half so tolerant of long-term human guests, who she would welcome with drinks and a delicious lunch when they arrived, then run out of energy and wish them gone by tea time. Not so with these feline incomers. The shopping bags grew heavier, the ever-whirring tin opener needed a new blade, and Mum kept smiling.

Strange to think that the Extras, mere bit-players in my own drama, may have cast a shadow decades later. This February, when I heard of the difficult circumstances in which Luna and Charles found themselves, perhaps a flap opened into some distant corner of my mind where three monochrome figures – they were all black and white - spend their days in unobtrusive harmony, purring an assurance that newbies always respond with gratitude for a new home, and respect the existing Cat in Residence.

Honestly! The unconscious can be shamelessly selective. Anyone would think I had never had to deal with the arrival of traumatised little Taboo. Anyone would think that every new cat in my life had been like Fish.

SHADOW CATS: FISH AND TABOO

How easy, as the Cycle of Cats revolves, to move back and forth in time. Type the word 'traumatised' in a paragraph referencing cats, and here she comes, tiptoeing into the light: troubled Taboo who joined our household after the waning of her beloved predecessor, Fish. And at the sound of her name, Fish leaps forth, twice the size and ten times as solid. Fish, the first cat who was entirely mine rather than a family pet, more central in my life even than Katy, let alone Jessica and the Extras.

It started with a card in the library. 'Spice, torti-white two year old female, very affectionate, free to good home'. I had just bought my first house, a little bow-windowed place on a hill with wild roses in the garden and views of green trees which belied the London postcode. It seemed a good home for a young cat. 'Very affectionate' sounded good for me, too. I had just ended a relationship (with a human being; there had been no feline in my life for the ten years I spent in a first floor flat), and though I had friends a few miles away there was nobody nearby, and it was lonely, in the house on the hill.

So I rang the number on the card and spoke to a pleasant man who invited me to his house a few streets away to meet Spice. Just an initial meeting, no strings, to see how we got on. It was like arranging a blind date. The family assembled in the hall to witness my introduction to their pet, who was sitting on the stairs, neither eager nor standoffish, but breezily friendly, much like her owner. Together, man and cat threw into relief the anxious expressions of the other humans: a very pregnant wife and a sweet little girl.

'Why are you letting her go?' I stretched out my fingers and received a sociable head-rub.

'The new baby,' said the man. 'Too much going on in this house. She needs somewhere quieter'.

Spice looked pretty chilled to me, and I probed further.

'Does she hunt?'

'Oh no. No, no, no', chorused the parents, while the little girl piped up:

'Yes she does mummy, in the summer she does, remember, all summer she did it last year, remember, there were those mice, and then that pigeon, and the frogs?'

'Ha ha ha', went the parents, waggling guilty eyebrows at me. 'Don't exaggerate, dear.'

I said yes anyway, the deal most likely having been signed in the library at the moment my brain registered the words 'very affectionate'. By the end of the visit we had not particularly bonded, but she seemed a nice enough cat, and the question of how I, with my phobia of any small creature either dead or suffering, would cope with the serial slaughter that clearly came as part of the package, was shelved for the present. The month was November, which would make staying indoors more attractive to a cat, and surely by now the most at-risk garden creatures would have flown South, or started hibernating, and there would be no nesting until the Spring. Perhaps

Spice would mellow with age, or maybe living with me would make her change.

Many a human blind date must lead to equally optimistic couplings.

Fish – it was her favourite food, and she loved playing with water, and she didn't either look like a 'Spice' or answer to it, so her name changed as soon as I got her home – Fish lived up to that first impression of being chilled. She seemed no more than perplexed by the sudden change of scene and company, and did not appear to be pining for her old life. After a thorough inspection of my house she contentedly sat on my knee or looked out of the window for the first two days, after which she became restive and began hammering at the outside doors. I had intended to keep her inside for the prescribed three weeks, but one evening I answered the door without checking her whereabouts and she shot past me, round the side of the house and up the back garden in the direction of her old home. After searching and calling for a few minutes, I had to sit and wait it out. A strange couple of hours those were. I liked Fish, but I didn't love her yet. I wanted her to come back safely, but if she didn't, my world would not be rocked. I had a premonition, sitting on the front steps as darkness quietly fell, that if she returned and we continued to live together, it would be a very different story.

She came back, unharmed and relaxed by the exercise, and the bonding process went ahead. One person and one cat living together can form something similar to a human couple (with some obvious differences!) and soon we were sharing a bed, getting up together, eating at the same times and dividing the responsibility, as far as was practical, for domestic duties. One night I was woken by a loud crash in or near the house, and could tell it wasn't a dream from Fish's response; we had both leapt to our feet before fully waking. I switched on the light and opened the door and we crept on to the landing; I leant over the bannister while Fish peered under it; side by side we made the journey down the stairs and into every room. We never discovered the source of the crash, but I was grateful for her company, though I can't think she would have been much use against any axe man lurking in the hall. It was the same when I hurt my neck and had to spend a week in bed, only tottering downstairs once a day to top up her water and biscuits. She couldn't offer cups of tea and painkillers, but she kept me company hour after hour, day and night, delighted to see me every time our eyes opened. Dear Fish, always there, and always there for me. I could even endure the horrors of the hunting season (the little girl had been right) for the pleasure of seeing her curled on my foot of my bed when I returned from burying the mangled remains of some unfortunate rodent.

When, four years later, I met Steve and he moved in with us, she accepted him calmly, but always remained my cat. There were two couples in the house on the hill, and I was a part of each of them. The arrangement worked beautifully, with Steve and Fish developing an easygoing friendliness. She had some idea of sitting on his knee while he watched television, but the first attempts coincided with particularly exciting football matches, and all the shouting and cheering and fist shaking and leaping to his feet permanently put her off. So it was still Fish and me tucked up together on the sofa of an evening, with Steve beside us.

Fish was the only cat whose name I deliberately changed. My therapist, intrigued by her significance in my life, saw past the rationalisations about calling her after her favourite food, and suggested she was named for the old secret sign for Christ, ICTHYS, which stood for faith and hope and whose letters were arranged in the shape of a fish. That may be so, but when Steve moved in, it was over his chippy supper that they bonded, the one he collected on his way home from work every Wednesday evening when I had a late therapy session. She would be waiting for him, he reported, on the front steps, and follow him into the kitchen where he would cut off a slice of steaming cod, remove the batter and flake it onto a saucer. By the time he had poured a drink and laid a place for himself, she would have finished her portion and be eyeing up his plate.

Come to think of it, there was something of the British Shorthair about this combination of single-minded devotion to one person with a general cordiality. Fish loved getting wet and playing with tap water, too, another Shorthair trait. She lacked the trademark good looks, she was a basic moggy, pretty only in the way that nearly all cats are pretty, off-white with uneven torti markings and fur just long enough to get everywhere without giving her the distinction of the 'longhair'. A very ordinary cat at whom you would not look twice if you passed her in the street, but a shining light in my life.

Always there for me, but possible to leave behind with a clear conscious – a rare combination. I could drop her off at the cattery and go on holiday knowing she would not just be safe, but happily occupied until I got back. Admittedly the cattery she attended was rather a special place, run and staffed by top-notch cat lovers. It was large, a number of chicken wire 'blocks' set in a huge garden, and thoughtfully organised. Each block contained individual runs, but also communal areas furnished with boxes and stools, and if you signed a disclaimer, your cat was allowed to mingle for a few hours each day. Because everyone was in transit, there was no time to get territorial, but if a cat showed signs of claiming sole rights to a shared space she was moved to another block, and as a last resort lost her rights to mingle, though this was rare. Staff and volunteers roamed amongst the residents, stroking and offering a knee when required. It was a kind of cat heaven.

I was charmed to see Fish interacting with her fellow felines, especially the time when I arrived to find her curled up in a disused rabbit hutch with a matching torti-white female with whom she had apparently spent the whole fortnight. I said her name and she glanced at me before snuggling back into her friend's fur. There was always an interlude after each long separation during which Fish didn't acknowledge me. People sometimes say their cats are 'sulking' or 'punishing them' for going away, but I think it's possible that for some cats, the process of recognising their humans takes a little time. On this occasion, we were in the taxi and nearly home before she looked up and gave a huge purr.

Fish gave no sign of missing her torti-white friend, but her holiday relationships showed that she was capable of affection towards other cats once the territorial difficulties were removed. I only wished she could have been so friendly to Princess, who lived next door and used to join me in my garden in pre-Fish days, but was not even allowed the use of her own patio from the moment Fish started going outdoors. Princess resigned herself to hurrying in through her own cat flap whenever Fish came out of hers, and I was relieved that no fisticuffs occurred. It is uncomfortable to be held responsible for the behaviour of a creature over whom you have no real control.

When Fish was eight years old, we moved house, a big deal for any cat. We booked three weeks in the cattery to spare her the disruption of the move and to lessen her ties with the old home, but I was still concerned to see how much harder she found the settling in process, even though this time she moved with familiar people. She had become slightly arthritic and lost some of her energy since I first met her, and her explorations of the new place were more tentative, her longing to get into the garden milder. Outside doors could be safely opened during the first couple of weeks without her shooting through them. When finally allowed out with my blessing, she took a few steps on to the patio and came back several times before scrambling over the fence next door. My heart froze, fearing she would try to make her way 'home' across two busy roads, but when I went upstairs and called from the bedroom window, she was soon back at my side. My sense of direction is terrible, and I admire the cat's internal satnav that takes her unerringly to the correct spot. Fish had never before seen the house from the outside, but could instantly locate the room that belonged to each window.

A Life Told In Cats

For a short time after Fish joined us at our new address, there was a curious change in my perception of the house and garden which I can only put down to a kind of telepathy. The new cat flap opened into a narrow side return, and I would keep seeing images of a long, high, rather scary tunnel with tall trees beyond it, which must have been how that area looked from 18 inches above ground-level. There were shallow steps into the lawned area, and I seemed to make a favourable comparison between them and a rocky ridge which corresponded to the terracing in our old, steep garden, which Fish had flown over in her younger years but must have found challenging when her arthritis was bad. A human being might have regarded this removal to a more level garden as a reasonable adjustment for a mild disability. I don't suppose Fish went that far, but I did sense a kind of appreciation alongside her apprehension at the unfamiliar contours of this new space.

It was a strange time. In a few weeks Fish found her confidence, to the point of starting a campaign of terror against Womble next door (poor Womble, the sweetest cat, black and white like Princess but a little more tenacious about standing his ground), and my strange cat's-eye view of the world faded away.

There were a few things about Fish I might have changed if possible; less hunting would have been an advantage, and a more neighbourly attitude, but - what a terrific cat. I don't have many pictures of her, it was before the days of the phone camera, the endless click click clicking which produces one good photo to twenty worthless blurs. There is a handful of snapshots from my little Nikon, when I remembered to get the films developed, and they all show Fish's face smiling up at me, her tail straight and proud. I have one that was taken on the penultimate day of her life, still interested and upright, though her body looks thin and her fur scrappy.

'There is only one death, the first', said Satre, and Fish's death was the first for me; worse than Katy's (I was not there) or Jessica's or Caz's (I heard about them from my dad, then widowed, and was sad mostly for him, left alone in the house). Fish was so much part of my inner world that I kind of forgot she was mortal, and when one summer I dropped her off at the cattery and mentioned that she would need plenty of water because she was drinking a lot, and the owner said 'kidney disease – she'll be with you another couple of years', I was stunned. Absolutely stunned. How could Fish not be with me forever, or at least until she grew as old as Katy and Jessica? She was only nine when the vet confirmed the informal diagnosis of the cattery owner, and the two-year prognosis, adding that she also had hyperthyroidism. I did what I could to maintain her quality of life for as long as possible – none of the tasteless protein-free mush in expensive tins recommended by the vet, but small portions of poached fish and the water it was cooked in to encourage her to drink, and homeopathy to top up the conventional drugs. She lived another four years, which I felt was a matter of pride for both of us, my beloved friend and companion until the end.

A Life Told In Cats

Fish's death was the first for me, and marked the first occasion I had to make the decision that faced me earlier this year, after losing Mia. The cat is dead; long live the cat. But which cat, and when? How to decide?

We took a holiday just after losing Fish, in Cornwall, a healing part of the world if ever there was one. While we were away I felt as close to her as I had during any other time away from home, but when we got back to the empty, empty house – I started to call her name when the front step was bare – I realised that we needed a cat in this house to turn it back into a home. Steve was about to start a job in the midlands and would be away during the week, and the loss of my entire household in one go felt too much to bear. Replacing Steve was not an option, but we should get a cat, any cat, as quickly as possible.

Well, almost any cat. There is something exciting as well as tragic about a pristine cat-shaped space readying itself to be filled. Changes can be made, or at least hoped for. Definitely a non-hunter would be easier this time, and perhaps one who responded less violently to having her tummy tickled by strangers – 'Vicious Fishus', someone called her, though she was always charming to me, except when picked up unexpectedly – OK, she could be feisty. One who got on better with the neighbours would be a relief – poor Womble, routinely attacked by Fish in his own garden, which she ruled as her own territory even though, like Princess, Womble was already established when we moved in. A prototype formed in my mind of a mild creature who'd lost her home through no fault of her own, possessed of an easy-going willingness to fit in with any other local felines (that would be the Extras again, casting their shadow). Surely that wouldn't be hard to find. But who cared. I was desperate. Any cat would do.

Steve was sad to lose Fish, but he recognised that my bond with her was deeper, and suggested that a few months of recuperation might be in order, following such a major loss, before attempting to replace the irreplaceable. He was right; I nodded and agreed quite sincerely before picking up the phone to make an appointment with the nearest rescue centre, the one in Catford (I liked that; almost as apposite as Catrina).

In fact, it was early even to visit the Centre, let alone bring home a new cat. We were met in reception by a tense volunteer in a stained tee shirt who demonstrated a weird lack of empathy for our situation, considering her role was to match cats with owners. She gave our living arrangements, habits, history and motives a thorough third degree before asking what we were looking for, then bristled at my request for a youngish cat who would not be likely to get ill or die too soon, because, I explained brokenly, it would take a while to feel ready to go through that again. And no actually, we didn't want to take on a pair, because we especially liked the kind of relationship that happens with an only-cat. I started to tell her about Fish, but the woman arched her back and narrowed her eyes and practically hissed at me.

'It's not all about you. These cats need somewhere to live. It's not very nice for them here, is it?'

She waved an outraged arm towards the minimum-legal-size wire cages, stacked four deep, in the stuffy room beyond the reception area. Having made us feel as bad as possible, she showed us around, ending up at a cage where a small slender tabby sat upright and watchful – eager to catch my eye, it seemed – and told us her story.

Tabitha, as the Centre named her, had been dropped off one evening by some geezer claiming that she was a feral living under his shed and that he personally hated cats and would never allow one in his home. ('In which case,' thundered the volunteer, 'why did he own a cat basket?' We could only shake our heads.) They accepted her without going through the usual paperwork because they feared for her safety with that man. She was only a few months old, barely ready to leave her mother, and the poor mite had now been at the Centre for eighteen months, during which time three attempts to rehome her had failed.

'What went wrong?' we dared to ask.

'Oh, she didn't settle. Anyway, she's the only one you can take on her own, if you insist on not homing a pair. She's scared of the other cats. She's lovely, though, aren't you, Tabitha…'

And truly, you would not have guessed her troubled past from the way she occupied that small clean cage, second from the left, top of the stack of four. Rescue centres were busy in those days, and you would think that the mogs would be frantic from over-crowding, but not Tabitha, who sat quite still, blinking shyly. Surely here was the gentle creature of my imaginings? Steve and I said we'd go away and think it over, as we'd agreed to do before coming in, but I think we both knew it was a done deal and so did the volunteer, who came close to smiling when she said goodbye.

Claire Entwistle

Tabitha! The name of the good witch's daughter in that American children's drama I used to watch, thinking how well it would suit a tabby cat. There was already something familiar about her. She was as small and as stripy as Katy, Katy in her early days, before she filled out. Katy, the centre of warmth in my young life.

She was also very similar to another Tabitha, a new arrival at the home of my therapist, Allan. What a coincidence! It seemed like fate! Again. Is there some law decreeing that any cat needing a home seems like fate? During Fish's last illness I had been exhaustively discussing cat thoughts and feelings in my sessions, which may have been why Allan broke his usual impenetrability to give me notice of this impending addition to his household, much as he had let me know the previous year that he was planning to move his consulting room upstairs. She duly arrived and Allan tried to introduce us in the hall as I came in one afternoon, but Tabitha was frying other fish at the time and streaked past me up the stairs, no more than a brown and cream blur.

It was an odd business. Having alerted me to her presence, Allan did not especially welcome my level of interest. 'You're talking as if you think I've got the cat for *you*'. I replied simply 'All cats are for me' – not that I believe I own them all, but their presence gives me something. A foot in the door, maybe. A cat in a house is something I can always connect to, whatever the difficulties with the human residents.

I never saw her again. Shortly after my own Tabitha moved in, I had a sense that Allan's wasn't there any more. A cat-less home it seemed that I came to for therapy, chilly and empty, and I said as much. After a few evasions, Allan admitted that there had been an unexpected allergy problem with 'one of his family' – perhaps he feared that I might ill-wish the hapless relative if he got more specific – and Tabitha had gone to live with his sister in Devon where she was very happy.

So much for his Tabitha, a lively soul whose allergy problem was quickly solved. Our Taboo, as she soon became known, was something else altogether. She left her upright posture and engaging expression back at the rescue centre and succumbed to what looked like full-blown PTSD. Released from her carrier into our kitchen-diner, she disappeared straight up the chimney, emerging at 3 am on the third sleepless (for me) night and tiptoeing towards the food bowl at the same moment I happened to come downstairs to check on her. Telepathic communication perhaps, but it did not extend to trust. I swiftly blocked the fireplace before she could get back up, whereupon she established HQ inside a rolled-up rug under the sofa where she stayed for weeks, only emerging to run round the edge of the room, screaming in a high voice and swishing her tail. It was like watching something out of The Exorcist. I suppose you could call it 'not settling'. I never saw her sleep or even lie down; she was either hidden in the depths of her rug, or bolt upright, poised for flight, or in manic motion.

With Steve working away from home, Taboo and I were on our own for much of this formative time. I would crouch beside the sofa calling gently, and after a while she would creep out and let me rub her head, purring with all the ease of an out-of-control chainsaw, before shooting off round the room again. Later came a stage when she would pause to sit on the dining room floor, but only while she was alone in there with the door closed. I knew it happened by the thump of that tail on the wooden boards. Thud, thud, thud. I would pause outside the door, reach for the handle and – whoosh. An empty room. Empty, but not cat-less. She left her mark, her energy in the air, quivering with promise.

The promise was what made it bearable; the promise and the hope, the tender signs of spring in the bleak winter of her young life. One morning I came downstairs to find her not under but on the sofa, and though she tensed at the sight of me, she stayed put. That night I left a blanket in that spot, and found hairs on it the next morning. Softly, softly, softly. There came a morning when she was on the blanket, stretching as I opened the door, then an evening when we looked up from the television to see an uncertain head appear around the door for a moment, then, several attempts and several hours later, her whole body.

The thaw continued a little faster. She ventured, step-by-step, upstairs. She inspected a windowsill. She allowed us to observe her sleeping, provided we kept our distance. She jumped on to my knee! Thud, thud, thud, went her tail against my leg, then she was off, but back the next day, for ten minutes this time, sitting bolt upright, covering Steve with an anxious green gaze, the thump of the tail fading to a soundless twitch.

And so, weeks later, we met again the upright, shy little tabby who first captured our hearts. I could only think that the limitations of the rescue centre had calmed her; four wire walls, a solid roof and ceiling, a small space into which food and water were placed by familiar hands, and waste removed. A place where nothing much happened. Perhaps the rehoming episodes, those exoduses into high-ceilinged expanses thick with unknown smells and sounds, were a source of terror, not hope. Yet still she had sat up straight at the first sound of our voices, and sought our eyes. There was, perhaps, a wish for change. I hoped so, because otherwise we had done her a disservice by moving her yet again. Steel bars do not a prison make, to misquote.

Observing Taboo's first sortie into her new garden, I agreed with the angry (though estimable) volunteer who disbelieved that man's claim that she had been living outside. Everything was new and terrifying. Head back, she stared with dilated eyes at the looming sky, ducking from every bird that passed overhead. Her first attempt was measurable in nanoseconds, but her second was longer and slower, and eventually she was lying on the patio like any other domestic tabby, the thumping tail no more than a flick of the tip, and our work was done – at least until the next time something triggered her trauma and the frenzy returned.

We learnt to anticipate the triggers and avoid them as far as possible by keeping her home life quiet and consistent. No chance of preventing next door's cat, Womble's more violent successor, from terrorising her in the garden (more about this later), but we could take measures to enable her to stay at home when we were away. For Taboo, the one time she attempted it, the cattery was a very different place from the holiday camp Fish used to love; a battleground of wire and wood and noise, controlled and populated by monsters. The staff stopped letting her into the communal area after she spent her first afternoon trembling on top of the highest shelf. They moved her into a corner run and provided a soft, hollow tube to hide inside, and her state of mind improved a little, but when we arrived to pick her up and saw her terrified eyes, we vowed that this 'holiday' would be her last, and that from now on feline staycations would be the order of the day.

I don't know. Maybe if we had persevered with the cattery a few more times she would have realised it was less dangerous than she feared and begun to enjoy it, just as she came to enjoy living with us. There were things that took a long time to become acceptable. She insisted for months that the cat flap was beyond her capacities, backing away when we stooped to demonstrate its mechanism and lurking behind the sofa while we crouched on the back step calling her and feeding scraps of chicken through the open flap. It was looking as though litter trays and on-demand door-opening were there to stay, until my great-nephews came to see her for the first time, hurtling towards the kitchen with shrieks of welcome, and suddenly there was Taboo on the other side of the French windows, heading for the fence.

This gave me pause. Had she known all along how to use the cat flap; was she afraid of seeming too capable in case we stopped helping her? Or was she simply enjoying having doors opened and litter trays provided for her convenience? Taboo's terror was indubitable most of the time, but there were little episodes of drama, especially as time went on. When we had the dining room floor replaced so that there was a divider where the kitchen tiles started, Taboo claimed to find this harmless strip of wood terrifying, hesitating on one side before taking a running leap right over it – except when she thought we weren't looking, when it mysteriously became an inoffensive section of floor. Even if there was a bit of exaggeration going on, it felt like progress, a sign that she could relate to and anticipate our responses, have some fun with them even, rather than being overwhelmed by fear.

Taboo's level of trauma had come as a shock to Steve and to me, especially as she arrived in the shadow of her gung-ho predecessor, but perhaps of all my cats, the unfolding of her life was the most satisfying and nourishing to witness: that long transformation, cactus-slow, from scaredy-cat to entitled diva. Five years later, far from cowering under sofas, she was insisting by means of squeaks and put-upon expressions that the fire be switched on for her comfort, or her favourite chair cleared of coats, or the blind raised a few inches so she could sit comfortably on the window sill. At night, her ecstatic purring and rolling on our pillows kept us awake, but however many times I sleepily scooped her up and dumped her by my feet, she would return to the head of the bed, rumbling with playful delight, entirely confident of our enduring affection and her own right to self-expression.

Taboo was not very long-lived, maybe ten when the all too familiar kidney disease took her, but what a life it had been. When Steve and I held her that last time at the vet's she looked up with what I am sure was deep, deep gratitude, which was fully returned. No doubt life with Taboo had been more challenging than my years with Fish, whose presence remained a delight and consolation, but who could have settled in almost any friendly household. With Taboo, it was different. We gave her a life, and she gave us the gift of giving a life.

A Life Told In Cats

WHEELS WITHIN WHEELS

The Cycle of Cats is multi-dimensional, with overlap, at times, between households. Fish and Womble, their fates joined and divided by a wooden fence, died within a week of each other. A strange coincidence considering the differences in age, health and cause of death. Despite her illness, Fish reached the respectable age of 13, but poor Womble was still young and fit. He disappeared one day and was discovered later to have ventured into the traffic on the South Circular Road. I sincerely hoped that he hadn't strayed so far in order to escape Fish's territorial terrorising. She never ceased defending the local gardens against Womble's inoffensive presence, even when poor health made it hard work. What was the point, Fish? Doing cat things, I suppose that was the point. Andy did his best to protect Womble, to the point of chucking small pebbles or water in Fish's direction when she came looking for trouble, but she only treated this as an extra challenge.

We didn't want to repeat this situation with the next cat, and thus Womble's gentle character influenced the search for Fish's successor. On his side of the fence, Andy mirrored our process by vowing to replace Womble with something more robust. The two households made their choices separately but ended up collecting the chosen ones on the same day, from the same rescue centre, in the same car, indeed, Steve having left London just before Taboo was ready for collection, so that Andy offered me a lift. Two tense cats in two carriers, side by side on the back seat, each behind the new human on whom their very existence would in future depend, starting new lives a few yards apart. Would they remember their common origins at the Centre, and start off as allies?

Nope. As soon as both had access to the outdoors, there began another reign of terror, this time Waldo's over Taboo. (Andy was sorry to lose the name 'Womble', his football team being Wimbledon, and the initial W kept the flame burning). A black bruiser with teeth we had reason to know carried some formidable bacteria, Waldo remained a hazard in Taboo's life till her last days. I never threw anything at him, liquid or solid, but I learnt to rush to our tabby's defence at the first sounds of yowling, and I hurled some pretty evil looks at his rear end as it disappeared over the fence and I stooped to examine the trembling stripy fur for teeth marks. One such incident necessitated several visits to the vet and a double course of antibiotics. We didn't have insurance, and spotting Waldo in the street on the way back from the final appointment, I found myself hissing 'You just cost us eighty quid'. He strolled on by.

Somehow we remained friendly with Andy and his partner throughout these episodes, discussing the feline situation and other issues of the day over the garden fence, and sometimes meeting for dinner or a game of bridge. They were lovely people who enhanced our lives, and we might not have got to know them so well without all that flying fur, however difficult it made life at times. We were all cat lovers together, you see. More to unite us than divide.

It was bizarre that, like Fish and Womble before them, Taboo and Waldo also waxed and waned in synch. Both died eight years later, not on the same day but within a couple of weeks of each other, and left each grieving household to ponder again what manner of cat should follow. None of the four humans concerned had especially enjoyed being responsible for either the aggressor or the preyed upon; was some third way to be found? Andy went back to the rescue centre and returned with Webster, a tuxedo sweetheart with a strapping physique and a mild manner. We, of course, chose British Shorthairs, known for their peaceful natures and their friendliness to animals and humans of all kinds. And indeed, when Mia and Poppy first met Webster in the garden, all was harmony, with rubbing of cheeks and touching of noses. Poppy, unsure how to judge this situation, looked for guidance to Mia, who kept inviting him into our house, so Poppy did likewise whenever she saw him. This led to some friction with Andy. 'You're not feeding Webster, are you?' he would enquire as I brought the bins in, and I could only assure him that although Webster often swung by for a few biscuits, it was without any human encouragement. Mia would turn up similarly uninvited in Andy's place, strolling through his French windows and up the stairs to take a snooze on his bed. I could think of no way of changing this situation, but in time the cats sorted it out between themselves. Mia developed some of the territorial instinct that had lain dormant during her years at the breeding place and also became more chary of people she didn't know well. Poppy followed suit, Webster did his own thing, and the visits, in both directions, ceased.

Webster was still alive and well six years ago when we left London and moved with Mia and Poppy up to Cumbria. I hope that this is still the case, and that his life did not end when Mia's did, especially as he was several years younger. Perhaps the fact that Poppy goes on will grant Webster some extra time. That really is fanciful... still, I think I will enquire, casually, in my Christmas card, about Webster's health.

Whether or not the demise of the first two pairs of feline neighbours can be regarded as more than coincidence, the personality of the moggy next door certainly influenced they way I chose the next incumbents, and therefore influenced my own life too, because I have been a different person with each cat. Steadied and cheered by Fish, challenged and affirmed by Taboo, relaxed and sweetly saddened by Mia, amused and intrigued by Poppy. Katy and Jessica and the Extras, and now Luna and Charles, have had still other effects. The jury is still out on the last two.

Then there are the human spheres spinning in this planetary dance, around and within the feline ones. Neighbours and acquaintances we have bonded or argued with, cat lovers or haters who have comforted or reviled us. Meteoric interventions from certain heavenly bodies such as those friends who brought Mia and Poppy from London to Cumbria for us – the whole trip just for that, starting and ending in Devon, because for various reasons it was not practical to drive them ourselves – and then, six years later, offered to transport Luna and Charles from Okehampton, *but only if it could happen that weekend.* Would we have gone ahead without their offer of help? Uncertain as we were, would we have been ready to make the commitment before the cats were snapped up by some other, closer connection? Who knows. In a classical play, Deb and Judy would be the Deus Ex Machina, the unseen element popping out of the machine (in this case a Volvo hatchback) to resolve a situation, then vanishing into the ether.

The course of a cat lover's orbit, coaxed by each new gravitational field, shifts and shifts again. Deb and Judy's ginger Jimmy died suddenly of a stroke around the same time as Mia, and when they were ready for a new cat and started experiencing in Devon the same problems I'd had in Cumbria, I determined to return the favour by helping in any way possible. They tried all the usual channels – went round to the local Blue Cross rescue place which had provided Jimmy, found it closed, and contacted other shelters. Some had cats ready for rehoming, allegedly, but there always some reason why Deb and Judy's offer was refused. The lived in a quiet Close beloved of dog walkers, not on but near a main road, and they had friends who sometimes brought their dogs to visit. For some organisations, one or more of these circumstances instantly debarred them. Also they went away quite often, which gained them a resounding NO before they could explain that family members close by, folk who would soon know the cats well and love them, were available to visit or live in for as long and as often as required. Eventually Deb started stretching the truth, implying if not actually saying that they rarely went out and received almost no visitors, and from then on they were only considered for very elderly animals, because they sounded so decrepit themselves.

It wasn't easy, but they persevered, and one day a call came through from a rehoming organisation willing to offer a moggy still in healthy middle age. The process could go ahead, all being well, after the obligatory house visit. How about Friday, or next Monday? Ah. There was no concealing the fact that they were just setting off for a two-month trip to America which belied all those careful description of their stay-at-home existence. Back to the drawing board.

I had my fingers crossed for them and kept making suggestions for things they had already tried, as people did to me when I was looking. And then, once again, Archers Cats came good. There was a post from a woman I knew through the group, and trusted (funny how quickly you sometimes get the measure of people you meet online), saying that a real-life friend of hers had rescued some young cats in Spain, and was willing to transport them to the UK if good homes could be found. There was a link to another Facebook page displaying some enticing photos.

After reading various horror stories about criminals using social media to advertise pets for sale, taking payment up front for animals whose photos turned out to be downloaded from stock image sites, I was cautious about this route, but after all it was Facebook that led me to flesh-and-blood Luna and Charles. My good feeling about this woman and her Spanish connections prevailed, and I put her in touch with my friends. The process was bizarrely more straightforward than going via the local rescue centre, and soon two white-and-grey beauties disembarked from the Plymouth ferry: Miguel and Carlos, named in that order because Miguel arrived, and remains, Chief Cat. Both were unphased by the changes of scene and language, and indeed by the visiting and neighbouring dogs, whom they regarded more as entertainment than predators. Their Spanish coats proved rather thin for the British weather, but that problem was solved by snuggling up together. So happy to be in their new human family and so sweetly affectionate with each other (if only Charles and Luna could manage that!), they will change the lives of my friends just as they have changed mine. And so on, round and round. The Music of the Spheres.

Today is a solemn occasion: September 19 2022, the funeral of Her Majesty Elizabeth II. On the Archers Cats page, the day has been set aside entirely for photos and tributes to cats who have died. So many of them, page after page, scrolling on and on and on. So many humans remembering so many cats with so much love, memories and thoughts and feelings circling the humans left behind, in and out, spinning and spiralling into the future. So much loss and renewal. The Queen is dead. Long live the King.

A Life Told In Cats

DARK SIDE OF THE MOON: LUNA

Queen Luna. Mia's successor, she of the propitious name, gleaming with meaning. Now, in September, seven months into her reign, it is time for a review.

Luna! How that name plays on my heartstrings, a riff I now remember first hearing last December, when Mia's light still illuminated our home. Scrolling through Facebook while Christmas shopping, an advert caught my eye: a young woman entranced by moon-like shapes in palest pink and blue.

Never trust a Facebook advert unless you have already had a good experience or a reliable recommendation for the company. I've been caught out so many times, ordering duvet covers in 'ethically produced linen', or some simple but sensational kitchen gadget that claims to cube a squash or open a tin without risking your carpel tunnel. The company website invariably ends '.co.uk' and boasts a generous returns window, but the item, when it turns up weeks later, is made from artificial fibre and incorrectly sized, or is no more than a pointless lump of plastic, made in and despatched from some sweatshop in China whither the aggrieved customer is required to return the package at her own expense.

My policy, now, is never to order anything I see advertised on Facebook by an unknown company, even if I need the item and love the photos. Instead I find the company on Trustpilot, scrolling past positive reviews which babble of exceptional quality and outstanding customer service. I study the negative reviews until a pattern emerges: the items delivered didn't match the photos or fell apart the first time they were used, or never arrived at all, or cost more to send back than to buy. Then I return to the Facebook advert and use the Comments section to report back to potential buyers. Sometimes the company deletes my comment immediately, sometimes not, but I hope to warn at least a few hapless consumers and stem the rising tide of exploitation.

Then I permanently hide all posts from this advertiser and block them from contacting me in future, whereupon the Facebook algorithm notes that I have interacted with purveyors of soi-disant sustainable bedding or cooking gizmos, and sends me another crop, and I repeat the process. I feel like Canute, but I keep going.

Despite all that bitter experience, this Lunar Calendar advert got under my skin. I thought Steve would love it, and if he didn't, I would keep it. Fifteen quid including postage was reasonable for an A4 calendar. So it was disappointing, the following week, to receive in the post a single sheet of paper in a plastic wallet. Seriously? I read the website again and found that indeed it promised no more, though the paper was classified 'high quality card'. Each month, rather than getting its own page divided into days, was represented by a scatter of small images, mostly circles: black for a new moon, black and white for the quarters and frosted colours for the full moons, with dates and names in a font inaccessible to the naked eye. Steve's birthday in January would be celebrated by the Wolf, which was shaded pale grey, and the Wolf sat next to the only non-circular image on the calendar, a cluster of three yellow shooting stars. 'Quadramid meteor shower' said the text, when consulted with a magnifying glass. OK, I had learnt something: that meteor showers, like moons, appear at predictable intervals and have names. I declared the sheet of high quality card an unworthy gift, put it on my desk where it proceeded to gather dust between a stray tape measure and a tub of dried-up biros, and chose a poetry book for Steve's present.

For those of us unable to sustain a truly Zen indifference to outcomes, life is full of disappointments, big and small. Luna, washed up on a Spring tide of expectations which, Canute-like again, I had struggled in vain to suppress – the reality of Luna is magnificent, but not quite the cat I was longing for. She's a Shorthair like Mia, but her first weeks reminded me more of Taboo, those endless explorations of the house, the starting at sudden noises, the refusal to sleep except out of human sight. Luna must have fitted in some naps, but for weeks we only saw her high-eared, poised for flight, flinching at any sound of human activity: a door closing in the hall or footsteps overheard. Happy day when Steve went downstairs one April morning to find Luna flat out on the kitchen table, barely stirring when he approached.

Did this landmark announce the end of her skittishness? Nope. Steve and I endlessly assured each other that these things take time as Luna continued to leap and growl and hiss at imagined threats, most worryingly at Poppy, half Luna's size, five times her age, coming peaceably downstairs for her breakfast. Poppy's claws are overgrown and she trots around like a little horse; impossible that her approach ever caught Luna off guard, but still Luna bristled and swelled at the sight of her not-so-new housemate. 'Oh my God,' you could almost hear her shriek, 'What the hell is that?'

Still. Shorthairs are tolerant and peaceful, we reminded ourselves. Luna has had a difficult time, all those losses and changes, but she'll soon revert to type. Charles is fine with Poppy, remember. But no, months later Luna was still doing her 'What the hell is that?' routine, and sometimes actually pouncing on Poppy, making her squeak and clatter away. But not every time! Sometimes she watched Poppy trot by with half-closed eyes, and as the weather grew warmer there were afternoons when all three cats lay out in the garden, lining up along the patio with a couple of meters in between, like a COVID queue. Not perfect, but better.

We had agreed from the beginning that Poppy would come first. If either of the new cats caused Poppy physical or mental damage, they would have to go. But no scabs or scars were in evidence. Once I walked into a confrontation on the stairs and caught Luna's punch on my bare leg: the softest thud of furry paw involving no claws and none of her considerable muscular strength. But still, it wasn't very nice.

Not very nice, and even more concerning when we noticed Charles coming in for similar treatment. He'd be walking past his sister and she'd snarl and leap on him, quite unprovoked, at least to human perception – you never really know, if you have two legs and opposing thumbs, what feline gauntlet has been thrown down by a sidewise look or an officiously-angled tail. Luna had lived with her brother all her life; what chance was there for Poppy if Luna was still attacking him?

Things got even worse when Charles caught the habit from his sister, and started launching his own attacks on poor Poppy. He would creep under or behind the furniture as Poppy wandered around the front room, marking his prey with his one good eye, then leaping out when she came close. Sometimes he tried the same thing on Luna, who would curse and swipe at him. Poppy never retaliated, making her his preferred target. I think that for him it was just a game, because he responded good-naturedly if I blew his cover. 'Hello Charles, there you are!' I would say loudly as Poppy approached his devilishly cunning hideout, and he would give up and roll over. Sometimes I picked him up mid-pounce and he purred in my arms and rubbed my face with his. I wouldn't have touched Katy in the middle of an attack, not without elbow-length gauntlets. Not Fish either; her fighting instinct was as sharp as her claws.

I felt pretty sure that this war on Poppy originated with Luna and that Charles was just copycatting, in his own personal way. Such un-British-Shorthair behaviour; what could be triggering it? There were times, dismally evoking the gloom of Mia's final months, when Luna was listless as well as irritable, hardly eating and vomiting if she did. Was she ill? The vet thought not, though her gums were inflamed, possibly due to a virus but possibly indicating tooth decay which could only be explored, under general anaesthetic, by intrusive procedures which would be a last resort. We had had our fill of these decisions. Long and dark and bleak did Mia's shadow fall, at those times.

Luna's real-life shape was also long and dark, and another source of disconsolance. One of the few things about Mia that I might have wished different was her uncanny resemblance to a lump of limestone. It didn't matter in London where blue-grey contrasted with red brick and green grass, but it posed a serious problem in South Lakeland, constructed on a limestone pavement and containing many walls and terraces of the same stone. Mia blended in perfectly, which was no joke when I needed to locate her quickly, like the first few times she was allowed outside, or when she was out when a storm blew up. Searching and calling, I was always spotting her in our front and back gardens, and in those of our neighbours. If and when a new cat joined our household, I used to think, it would be a relief to have one that stood out better. Like Poppy for instance – was not white and orange once a standard for prison uniforms?

Charles's pale beige fits this bill; as well as having a different tone from the local rock, he glows helpfully in car headlights. But Luna's fur, deep ash and broken up by faint stripes, is even harder to spot than Mia's, especially when her back is turned and that long luxurious tail hangs down. Oh, Luna has a dark side, like her namesake. I wish she would stop attacking Poppy and Charles. I wish I knew why she did it. I wish I knew whether or not she's ill. I wish I could love her like I loved Mia, and that she returned my feelings. Why can't I? Why can't she?

'Dark' sounds sinister, but it only means 'unknown'. The moon shows one side of herself to the earth, and we call the other side 'dark', though it sees the sun just as often. How is this possible, when the moon, like the earth, is in constant motion? Because she rotates synchronously with the earth. When we move, she moves, presenting to us always the same face. It sounds like the sort of thing a cat might do, as you creep forward to examine an injured paw or pop a tablet between apparently sleeping jaws; there's a shift, and you are presented with the part of the cat she chooses you to see, or with nothing, as she melts away. Maybe the analogy holds the answer, which is prosaic enough. We always see the same side of the moon, but how different she looks at different times of the month, and Luna is different too at different times, and maybe that is all there is to say. Maybe she is roused to ill temper by causes opaque to the human observer, however concerned. Maybe some of these triggers are out of her control. The moon would know, she who exerts her greatest influence on the tide when she finds herself in line with other heavenly bodies.

There's a thought. It is common knowledge that creatures of all kinds are affected by the phases of the moon, and not fanciful to believe that a cat who happens to share her name might be one of them. I need to keep a diary for a couple of months charting her edginess against the images on my lunar calendar. I'll do it! It's not as if I had anything else to do, or as if there were more pressing matters in the wider world. I'd like to understand her better. I knew where I was with Katie's self-seeking and Taboo's chaos and Fish's steady affection. I knew where I was with Mia's clear, intelligent love which still shines from the shadows on to her shady successor. Luna's love is so changeable, head rubs and adoring looks alternating with cold shoulders and turned backs, not like Charles, always ready with a cheery purr, or Poppy, dancing within the orbit of a friendly hand. Luna is not typical of any British Shorthair I have ever met or heard of. On her more aggressive days I've catastrophised that I was sold a pup, as it were, and that Luna's blood is tainted by more irascible stock, a black mamba's perhaps, or a TV chef's. Or perhaps, in my blind acceptance of the British Shorthair 'brand', I have been fooled by the cat fancier's equivalent of the dodgy internet advert. Perhaps I should look up British Shorthair on Trustpilot, and start leaving comments for future punters on the breed's Facebook feed.

Speaking of which, I have a comment for the small business that makes the lunar calendars. I was walking down to the prom one evening with a friend, just as night was falling, and she gasped and said 'What's that?', pointing to a flat-bottomed disc in vibrant lilac-pink, huge and glowing at the edge of the sea. 'Is it a balloon? Is it the sun going down?' 'No,' I said, 'it's the moon'. We stood together and gazed as it gathered itself into a complete circle and floated into the sky. It followed us home, this pink moon, and I remembered the single-sheet calendar sitting on my desk. The month was August, and the corresponding circle was shaded exactly the soft and beautiful lilac-pink we had seen bobbing on the dark horizon. Sturgeon moon, it was named by Native American fishing tribes, because it appeared at the same time as an abundance of fish. A pink moon. Who would have thought. And soon to be followed by shooting stars.

Claire Entwistle

The lunar calendar has started to fulfil my hopes, now I understand it better, and perhaps Luna, my hopes for her, will turn out the same way. What an outrageous thing to think, let alone write, as if Luna only existed to make me happy! I'm reminded of the story of 'A Street Cat Called Bob' who, injured and straying, was rescued by James, a homeless busker addicted to heroin, and became his lifelong companion, lending his human friend a sense of purpose which turned both their lives around. Images went viral of ginger Bob sitting proudly on James's shoulder or snoozing on a blanket while James sang for their supper. Offers of assistance with recovery and housing and cat food flowed in, and, more bizarrely, offers of large sums of money to buy Bob. As if! Of course James refused, but any true cat lover would know that the Bob these folk were bidding for was not for sale. Most likely the item purchased would turn out to be an unsociable moggy, not in the first flush of youth, who would have pooed on the furniture and made endless attempts to return to his old life. What they really wanted to buy was the relationship, and you only get a relationship by relating.

You only get a relationship by relating. Maybe the dark side is mine, not Luna's. Maybe she wonders, in whatever way cats wonder, why I am so changeable, why sometimes I serenade her and scoop her up in my arms, and sometimes I look sadly past her as though at some other, more wondrous creature. Maybe in some wider, unseeable dimension, we might have a relationship as rich and loving as the one I had with Mia. Maybe that is possible. But at this moment, in this phase of the Cycle, it feels like crying for the moon.

BRAVE SIR POPPY

And what of Poppy, our hopes and fears for her? Did we do the right thing by her? We could, perhaps should, given how things turned out, have allowed her to live out her days in single-cat comfort, but there were some reasonably reasonable reasons for what we did instead. It was sad to see her listless and sleepy and alone without Mia to follow and copy, sad to see a day go by without her leading Steve downstairs for a stroke, sad to recognise that she would not be seizing the opportunity to curl up on my knee in the evenings as she'd so envied Mia doing. She lost interest in life, it seemed, was falling into depression, and we could not let that happen.

It seemed reasonable enough to believe – hope – guess - that a home in which other cats were present might be familiar enough, stimulating enough, to bring her back to her old self, if only by presenting the kind of challenges particular to cats. Poppy loves Steve and me, but we're a different species. Would the average person, accustomed to live amongst other humans, be happy to spend their old age exclusively with another life form, however well disposed?

It will be clear by now that if we thought Luna or Charles might take on Mia's role for Poppy, our hopes were misplaced. Poppy was heartbreakingly ready at first to be friends, approaching the newbies with a firm tread and settling a respectful few feet away, head on one side. Charles looked intrigued and lay down to return her gaze, but Luna just yowled – long high shrieks of dismay – until we lifted one of them up and took her away. We did not blame ourselves; we did the introductions by the book, getting them used to each others' scent, arranging brief, controlled meetings, fixing doors open a crack so they could observe each other safely, offering a special treat when they met to establish a happy association with the other cat. At times we seemed to be making progress, but then it would start again, Luna or Charles or sometimes both of them blocking poor Poppy whichever way she turned, or yowling and hissing, or pouncing on her.

Nothing in Poppy's earlier life could have prepared her for this. I visited the breeder's several times and despite the rather crowded conditions saw no signs of strife. The 'girls' formed a sociable team headed up by Mia, whose retirement Poppy had the honour of sharing. When they joined us in London there was friendly Webster next door and catless households on the rest of our section of road, most unusually for London. Our town in Cumbria is more popular with dog owners, and feline intrusions are rare here too. On the few occasions Poppy came across a strange cat in the garden, she would look around for Mia, who somehow always knew what was going on and would turn up, throw Poppy one glance of incredulous disgust, and do whatever was required by way of chasing, growling, or simply facing up to the intruder for as long as it took, taking a single tiny step every few minutes according to some code which Mia instantly accessed after a lifetime in captivity. Poppy would meanwhile lie on the ground and roll around with her paws in the air, possibly indicating submission, but more likely just relaxing in the knowledge that the problem was dealt with.

That was Poppy in the old days. So it was impressive that in her fourteenth year, unsupported and unguided, meeting spitting strangers on the stairs, Poppy remained calm, waited for them to subside and walked steadily past. After a while, she began to assess the danger under the table or in the hall and to hurry past Luna in an arc – a deep instinct that, and one she drew on directly, without Mia's example. Subject to sudden ambush, she trotted away a short distance, then sat down on her stairs, or in her kitchen, solidly claiming her right to be there. Just occasionally she retaliated. One morning, watching the two females crossing at close quarters in the kitchen doorway, I distinctly heard not one but two hisses, much like the brief interaction of two hostile humans passing in the street.

'Eff off'.

'No, you eff off'.

Poppy, again untaught, developed her own tactics for dealing with Charles. His favourite place for sleeping and chilling out remained for a long time the front room which was his and Luna's territory while they were settling in, furnished with bowls of water and biscuits and their litter tray. Poppy, who was previously quite happy to go in the garden for her ablutions, made a point of starting her morning by walking right round this room, occupied or not, spending some time in the sunny spot under the window, and using the litter tray. Twice, if Charles was being particularly frisky. Quite something for one whose breeder insisted that she could only be homed with another cat who would show her how to behave. The newbies didn't take over Mia's managerial role but offered something different and perhaps more precious: they put Poppy in touch with her own cat nature, her own British Shorthair nature.

It hasn't been easy, and I can't, hand on heart, say I'm certain that we did the best thing for Poppy. At times she still looks stressed, and we fear it is all too much for her, but she also looks interested, engaged. No more day-long snoozes in a solitary study. Would this change have happened anyway, as Steve and I recovered from Mia's loss and Poppy got used to being the only cat? Who knows, but I'm fairly sure that it is the constant competition that leads her to seek out her human friends and lay claim to her share of attention, whatever hissing or pouncing monster might stand in her way. Gold standard Shorthair behaviour. *Gallant* behaviour. 'Brave Sir Poppy', we call her, and she catches our admiring tone (I concede that she will have missed the cultural reference), and sits up straighter and tilts her chin for a rub. A fine cat indeed, in her own small way the best of the bunch.

FOR GOOD OR ILL

'First Do No Harm'. The Hippocratic Oath, though misquoted. Even doctors do not promise to prioritise 'doing no harm' nowadays, and cats take no oaths of any kind, for obvious reasons. Nor do cat owners, though some non-cat-lovers believe that we should pay more attention to, and swear to avoid, the harm that may result from keeping semi-domesticated animals in our homes. The taxi driver who haunts my conscience might have had something to say on that one. Not just that pets absorb resources needed by vulnerable humans, but that they actively do damage.

As a pet-owner I am inclined to think first about dangers *to* my pets rather than damage *by* them. I can see that this might be irritating to those humans who don't share my taste in domestic animals, and it feels awkward when, for example, our cats declare part of a neighbour's garden a toilet zone and act accordingly. I have offered to remove the results, daily if necessary, but nobody wants me stomping around their flowerbeds every morning, and there isn't much else I can do, except offer more desirable facilities in our own garden and hope that the neighbours concerned will deal kindly with the cats concerned. We are fortunate in the neighbours we have at the moment, but I'm not complacent.

Recently a notice went up on a nearby lamppost which offered a different perspective. 'Lost Pet' said the large print. This usually means a cat, but a closer look revealed a photo of a young woman draping a snake round her neck. Round her neck, then a glistening loop of reptile hanging down before its head appeared, resting on the girl's hand. From the opposite shoulder, a tail trailing right down to the floor… and along the floor... Dear God! It must have been eight foot long at least, and a foot in diameter.

I read with horror that this creature had escaped from a nearby house and the owners were 'concerned about danger from traffic.' Anyone who 'saw or heard anything' should ring the number at the bottom of the page. The family missed their beloved snake who would be getting cold and lonely.

There was no mention of how dangerous this creature might be to local humans or pets, and no apology for the worry to neighbours. Even more concerning was the fact that the poster was not laminated, so it would be unreadable after the first shower. The flimsy A4 sheet had already been scribbled on, the phone number obscured by a pencilled 'wrong number'. OK, so these folk without the nonce even to carry out a successful poster campaign, who showed no evidence of mounting a proper search nearby, were in sole charge of a Burmese python which was – I whipped out my smartphone - one of the five deadliest snakes in the world, to both humans and other animals. I hurried home making plans. We'd have to keep the cats indoors until the snake was found; Charles anyway, who was always sniffing around in undergrowth, and maybe Luna. Poppy stayed closer to home and was less curious, but was the least equipped to protect herself… And this could go on for weeks, assuming the snake was ever found! The poster didn't even explain how to check up on the progress of the search. The only contact details were a first name and the incorrect phone number, and the family could not even have been checking that the poster was still there, because they hadn't seen the 'wrong number' message and made a correction.

Hang on. They'd put a wrong number and there was no other way of identifying them… Yes, it was a hoax. Our excellent local councillor Fiona was on the case, and it was soon confirmed that the photo was filched from a website in the US and that our local vets knew nothing of a local python. Thank God, but why? Why pull such a pointless and alarming stunt on our neighbourhood, unless perhaps to upset the innocent woman whose phone number appeared on the poster and had been bombarded with irate or frantic messages?

Burmese pythons, which can (and do, according to Google) strangle or suffocate a grown man in less than two minutes, are of a different order than cats who occasionally kill small rodents, but that evening I got a whiff of how a wildlife enthusiast might feel about cats being allowed outside. 'If you must keep one – and why you would want to live with such a creature I cannot imagine! – at least keep it under control.'

I honestly feel very bad about the wildlife that suffers at the teeth and claws of my feline friends. Very bad, especially about the birds. Mice and rats living indoors feel like fair game, but little fledglings already under threat from climate change and loss of habitat, whose mothers desperately call them from above – those are something else.

A Life Told In Cats

I rejoice whenever the Cycle of Cats grants me a non-birding, non-mousing, non-frogging specimen. Frogs, ugh. They were the worse of Fish's offerings, one grim summer before Steve provided backup with the corpses and entrails. Backup, I say; he took over completely, along with putting out the rubbish and digging the garden. Those frogs were the worst, and certain unidentifiable, hopefully non-flying objects that Fish laid out on the dining room floor. One was just a blooded skull with a miniature spine dangling from it. Do frogs have spines? This kind of question I do not want to explore empirically.

I didn't blame Fish. She had a killer instinct, she was a carnivore, her ancestors roamed the plains way before the evolution of tins and pouches and addictive treats. I didn't even blame her for playing with her live prey, horrifying though it was to witness; she was simply honing her skills for the day when civilisation would be over, and a dormouse all that stood between her and extinction. I didn't blame her for involving me in her games, not even the time she threw a dead pigeon on to my lap in the garden, or the other time I was lying on the hearthrug chatting on the phone to my line manager, and received a still-warm mouse on the side of my mouth.

Did I blame myself for providing the means for her to abuse our fellow creatures in this way? Yes, I felt guilty and responsible and tried to stop her. I attached a collar and bell, but she disappeared into the bushes and came back without them. No point in repeating that exercise; she'd remove it again, and it might not help anyway. Katy, similarly shackled before the days of elasticated safety collars, had perfected a nun-like smoothness of gait that prevented the bell from ringing, and Fish was at least as clever as Katy. I tried keeping her inside at the most vulnerable times of year, but she was so desperate to get out, pawing at the locked cat flap and closed windows, that I gave in. Once a cat has the taste for outdoor life, it is cruel to keep her inside, making a prison of her home. Not for nothing is house arrest a human punishment.

Did I blame myself for putting my cat's needs before those of the local wildlife? Yes, but not enough to make me stress out my feline friend by restricting her freedom. Instead I hung around the garden waving my arms at low-flying birds like an automated scarecrow, until eventually they got the message and there were no more feathers on the dining room floor.

I've been quite fortunate in the proportion of non-hunters in my cat cycle. Katy hunted, but not Jessica. Fish, but not Taboo. Mia, but not Poppy. Fifty-fifty up to that point, so logically the next pair should include one of each. Luna of the springy legs and alert expression looked like a natural, so when be-whiskered corpses started appearing around the house as the spring wore on, I assumed she was responsible, and crossed my fingers that Charles would prove either incapable or uninterested in joining her. His monocular vision must be a hindrance to hunting, I surmised, and his elaborate stalking of Poppy, creeping on his belly under sofas and flattening himself behind curtains the better to surprise her, was surely a piece of theatre no rodent would have reason to dread.

It took a while to confirm this theory, because there were none of the forcible presentations that were Fish's grisly speciality, and none of the self-congratulation that Katy and Mia both indulged in when they made a catch, that particular style of purring and preening that makes you put on your shoes and the light before venturing into the hall. Nothing like that happened this time, no suspicious rustling, just two young cats looking much as usual, plus a dead body on the kitchen floor which Poppy would step around on her way to the garden, her gaze averted like a motorist avoiding an accident.

We live in an old house surrounded by undergrowth, with multiple gaps behind walls and under floors, so mice infestations are a recurring problem, and I hoped that the corpses represented pest-control within the home rather than the decimation of garden-dwellers. Only two birds turned up that spring, one an adult that had probably been picked up when already dead or badly injured, the other a plump fledgling which we actually saw Luna bring in through the cat flap and place on the floor near the sink. As I'd suspected, here was our hunter! I snatched her up and shut her in another room, then repeated the process with an interested Charles before checking the victim for signs of life. It was lying very still, but when manoeuvred on to a piece of cardboard, it turned its head a fraction. Poor little love! Should we put it out of its misery? (the plural pronoun is employed loosely here). Out of the question to return it in this immobilised state to the garden, where another predator would find it even if we kept ours shut in.

Google, consulted in some desperation, advised taking injured wildlife to the local vet, but doubting that they would welcome a call on a Sunday evening, we followed the alternative instructions – make a 'nest' for the bird, keep it in the dark, and it might, if not seriously injured, recover after a few hours. I filled a shallow cardboard box with dried leaves and some grated apple for nourishment and hydration, Steve added the fledgling, and the whole thing went into a larger box in which a coffee table had been delivered, taped up to keep the light out. The night seemed long, but come the morning the little bird was still alive, still turning its head, but not attempting to fly. Was it injured? In pain?

What a relief to have professionals at hand, equipped and skilled to relieve or end suffering, acting with compassion and humour and nerves of steel. Our local practice recently won a national award, and quite rightly. The receptionist blinked at the sight of the huge cardboard box when we manhandled it on to the counter – 'how big did you say this bird was?' – and giggled when I solemnly held my fingers a couple of inches apart. The vet would examine the patient, she said, and put it to sleep if there was no hope, but otherwise they would treat any injuries then transport it to Kendal College which had a unit for wild creatures. They would let us know the outcome.

We didn't blame Luna or Charles, whichever it was, and we certainly didn't blame Poppy, but it was uncomfortable watching our feline friends going about their contented business while that poor baby languished in a strange sterile place. The phone didn't ring until 4pm, and the nurse sounded rather brusque. The bird had turned out to be uninjured, they'd fed it, and now it was causing a nuisance flying about.

A Life Told In Cats

'We don't have anywhere to put it except a kennel, and it's taking up valuable space. Can you please come and collect your bird now, and put it back where you found it?'

Astonishing. It had been in Luna's *mouth*, between or at least close to her tiger-sharp incisors. She had placed it gently on the floor, then Charles had hurried over…

Steve went to collect the bird while I shut the two suspects in the front room and made sure Poppy was asleep upstairs. Luna had dozed off by the time Steve got back. He released the bird in the front garden, watched from the window by me and an intent, silent Charles.

Charles! Yes, he was the great hunter. I caught him in the act the following weekend; a flash of pale fur in the darkest corner of the kitchen, a tiny shriek from his direction but not in his voice, and he strolled past me with one of his affable purrs, leaving behind a still-warm corpse.

Luna, stretched on the kitchen table with her head on the butter dish, barely stirred. This was no hunter. 'Did you bring that bird inside to keep it safe? You can tell me,' I whispered, but she shut her eyes tighter. She was no pacifist, but no hunter either. The fifty-fifty rule held good. The Cycle of Cats spun on.

And what of the good done by cats? Consider, fellow cat-lovers, what percentage of your time is spent endeavouring to keep your moggy happy and well, and how you feel when you succeed. Your days, or at least the hours you spend at home, are all about giving and receiving, receiving and giving, and while your behaviour centres around making the cat happy, a stream of small rewards makes you happy too. A purr, which scientists say vibrates at just the level to promote human healing. A stroke, which calms your nerves as well as hers; perhaps a reciprocal rub of your leg so that you get stroked too. And food: a cleared bowl gives satisfaction, while a spurned meal presents a small challenge and a reminder that you are in the presence of a being with her own mind. Why, Luna, when we have just ordered a job lot of that chicken thing you liked so much last week, will you only eat the salmon one? OK, OK, here you are.

It's funny as well as annoying. On Archers Cats, stories like this are constantly exchanged, evoking nods and chuckles. 'Because, Cat,' people say, and offer an anecdote of their own. My own favourite story at the moment concerns Charles's attempt to find a cool spot during a spell of hot weather. Unknown to me, he chose the space next to the toilet in the upstairs bathroom, hidden from sight by the shower cubicle. In the evening I went in there and switched on the light, whereupon Charles started to purr loudly, only stopping when I left the room. I seriously thought, 'I didn't think we ever put an extractor fan in there…' and went back to see what was going on, once more switching the purr on with the light. I laughed out loud (literally, not just in the emoji sense) the first time it happened, and smiled each time the sequence replayed on subsequent visits to the bathroom, and laughed again recounting the story to friends.

What could be more therapeutic than frequent laughter, and kindly fun to share with like-minded folk?

A Life Told In Cats

Cats are funny, and they look after their own interests, and I find that heartening too. You can't train a cat. You can scare her, but it's not the same thing at all. You can show her a game that she'll remember and repeat, provided she enjoys it. You can teach her to associate certain events with treats - Luna races to the spot in the garden where I brush her, knowing that brushing means an Applaws Tuna Puree snack (allegedly 100% natural, so why is this plastic-coated teaspoonful of extravagance so much more attractive than a piece of fresh fish …?) – but I don't call that training either. I call it having a good memory.

Training is for dogs, in my opinion. Playing Articulate with Steve one Christmas, I instantly understood his clue 'opposite of cat'. Dog! A fine species, but very much not a cat. A dog takes pride and pleasure in following your instructions, however pointless. A cat may do what you ask sometimes, but you really shouldn't count on it. When you come home a cat may be pleased, delighted even, to see you, but not to the slavering, convulsive, whole-body-experience level of a dog, which can be quite painful to witness. I don't know how dog owners manage to go to work or have a social life (except in parks and certain pubs) while their animal friend pines at home. It must be hard enough putting the dustbin out.

Cats have needs too, and they expect you to fulfil them, but it all happens at a lower and for me more tolerable level. A dog wanting to go out (and they always want to go out) leaps and cavorts and brings you his lead. A cat with the same desire sits by the back door, not even looking in your direction, until you find you have stood up to open the door for her, even though there is a cat flap and even though you know she will be unsure, when faced with the chilly night air, that she wants to go at all.

Dogs are wonderful, if you can stand being rapturously welcomed every two minutes, and all the rainy walks, and the muddy fur that they don't clean themselves, and the poop-scooping. They are huge-hearted, glorious creatures and I have no wish to set them in competition with my species of choice. All pets, where the relationship is loving, can do us so much good: the companionship, the focusing of our warm attention on a creature that we can help and make happy, which is not always the case with human loved ones, especially adult children.

Parents are usually proud of their children, and though I don't call myself 'mummy' to my cats, I take a rather similar pride in them, as though their triumphs were mine. Mia was exceptionally beautiful, almost everyone said so, apart from the odd cat-hater, one of whom actually shrieked, meeting her for the first time, 'ugh, is that a cat, it looks like one of those rag rugs'. Oof! It was shedding season, and I was having trouble introducing her to the brush... But, shocking exceptions aside, most people were drawn to Mia's beauty and her way of being. Workmen would observe her observing them, and think it worth reporting back: 'she sat there watching me the whole morning, and when I finished, she came over to check out what I'd done...' Two guys delivering a fridge dropped it in the hall and headed, uninvited, into the front room where Mia was resting on the sofa. 'Is that a British Blue? I've only seen photos...' It feels a bit special, owning a pedigree; I say this with a degree of self-disgust because non-pedigree moggies can be just as lovely and interesting, and some pure-breds are far from universally appealing, for instance those shiny shivering creatures with no fur....

I knew, really, that it was not I but Mia was who was possessed of the orange eyes and smoky fur and winning ways; my sole contribution to her presence in our home was making some phone calls and collecting her from Orpington and paying for a lot of cat food; but whenever anyone's eyes lit up at the sight of her, I felt as pleased and proud as if some version of those attributes were my own. Surely if people admired my cat they would like me too? Love me, love my dog. Admire my cat, admire me.

I saw Allan, on and off, for many years, and he was a welcome piece of ballast in my life when Fish died and her place was filled by Taboo, then again when Taboo faded and Mia appeared. Observing the devastation of that first death, Allan suggested that rather than seeking to replace her with another cat, I might seek to embody the qualities that Fish represented. I just laughed. I had never known any human being, let alone myself, consistently display such single-minded devotion, such cheerful courage, such a contented, undemanding yet engaged relationship with life. Sure, I would have loved to be like her, but I would not have known where to start.

It was another matter with Taboo. All that rushing around and screeching and hiding – I can't say I never behave like that when things get tricky, but I certainly didn't want to do more of it, or to gain a reputation as such. The time we came to collect Taboo from her first and only sojourn at the cattery, I overheard a staff member remark, 'That couple's new cat is nothing like their last one,' and I felt really sad, not for the cats this time, but for myself. I had enjoyed being the purveyor of confident sociability in the shape of Fish, and did not welcome my new manifestation as trembling scaredy-cat, fond though I was of Taboo.

Just as I feel proud when my cat is praised, I feel quite defensive when people object to her behaviour.

'She is just doing what she needs to do', I feel like saying, if eyebrows are raised. 'She has already accommodated herself to living with us; give her a break if she doesn't always fit in perfectly. You're asking me why I let my cat on the kitchen table. I don't 'let' her, I just don't endlessly lift her off, in the knowledge that she'll jump up again ten seconds later. We all need to choose our battles.'

It's as if some people believe you can force your cat to act in certain ways. You can't, except by using barrier methods which may not work in your favour. You can shut her out of the kitchen, if you find that convenient, which we would not, given that the cat flap is in the back door; but once she's there you can't stop her jumping on the table, except perhaps by moving it into the next room, shutting the door and calling it the hall table.

Mia and Luna are inveterate sitters on, and walkers over, the kitchen table, even when it is in use by humans, and neither is above helping herself to the contents of our plates. I wonder if they are lacking some vital nutrient present only in grilled salmon or yoghurt or (in Luna's case) potato crisps. 'Were' and 'are', I should say, but the resemblance in their behaviour is so striking that I have to remind myself that it is not contemporaneous. Poppy has never got on the table. Charles goes up there occasionally, but only to snooze on the blanket at the end which has been designated for feline use. We treat all the cats the same, but they all behave differently. The same phenomenon is observable in human families.

Poppy, with her flat ears and comical expression and nervous demeanour, attracts attention of another kind, not censorious, but more humorous than admiring. I'm pleased when she makes a human friend, but she's always been more Steve's cat than mine, and I haven't felt so represented by her. Not by Katy either, back in the day. It was nice when strangers said 'what a pretty cat', but I didn't take credit for it, especially since their next word was usually 'ouch' as the indignant admirer snatched back a bleeding hand. The same with the other family cats. As a young adult, I invited home friends who loved playing with Jessica, but I never shared a home with her long-term, so we never bonded strongly. The credit for her winning ways all reflected on to my parents, and I often saw them proudly watching her antics and enjoying how people responded.

In a way, we *are* the cats we truly bond with, and there is a more serious side to this level of identification. 'Remember every day that you must die,' goes the saying; a teaching which is present in many faiths, and part of the Buddhist route to acceptance and peace. The Cycle of Cats inexorably, patiently, teaches us the shortness of life, not only theirs, but our own. If my cat moves every day closer to death, so do I. If I have to make hard decisions about the way her life ends, so I may have to one day for my human loved ones, and for myself.

I've heard parents of young children speak of getting a family pet to introduce their little ones to death in a way less painful than would happen through the loss of a friend or relative. I'm not sure of the logic of this when to the child, the pet may soon become a best friend or favourite family member, or both. Leave it to the grown ups to know, really know, that the time of the new moon – the dark phase when she grants no light to the black night sky – is a natural occurrence, decreed in the Cycle of Cats not by some predictable shifting of the planets, but by gravitational forces beyond our field of vision. Dark times may come out of the blue, but always as part of the Cycle. I'm at the edge of one now. A milky crescent of waxing moon glimmers beyond the clouds.

A Life Told In Cats

WHAT ABOUT CHARLES?

Charles almost didn't get his own chapter. I forgot about him when handing out the headings, as though some general remarks and guest appearances in Poppy's and Luna's stories were all he deserved. An interesting omission, especially at a time when his name is being spoken all over the world and we Brits adjust to having a new monarch. Long live the KING! Send HIM victorious! A new face on our coins, facing to the left after 70 years of right facing profile. 'CR' coming soon on police helmets. Barristers declared 'KCs'. Monumental changes, at a time of national and international grief. How long until the new language seems normal?

This year's losses and gains to the feline population of my home are hardly comparable, but it feels significant to have a male cat in residence. It has never happened to me before. Katy was Katy and the trend continued; Jessica, the Extras and so on, all females. As a small child I got the impression that all cats were female and all dogs male; one of those bits of nonsense that are hard to let go in the face of later evidence. And Tom, the exception to the cats-are-girls rule, was not very nice to Jerry.

When it was a question of finding a friend for Poppy, I was advised by several folk with experience to choose a male, because he would be more likely to get on with a female. Alfie certainly seemed at home in the Girls' lodge in Orpington. But I never seriously considered a male. Some of my reluctance was based on the well-publicised problems of keeping a tom cat, or failing to 'keep' one, because he will be off all the time looking for nookie and getting into trouble. Once neutered, the likelihood of this kind of behaviour is reduced, but not eliminated. Friends with male cats report that they have larger territories and bloodier fights. Males are more likely to spray than females, sending upwards and outwards that hideous smell that is even worse than ordinary cat urine; and, on that subject, if a male develops a UTI, the consequences can be much more serious. The list goes on, creating a bias towards females in my logical brain, never mind what my unconscious is up to, pursuing the goddess archetype or whatever.

Then Luna turned up with Charles, the delicate child of the litter, and suddenly we have a male in our midst. He doesn't spray, thank God, and shows no signs of urinary discomfort. Nothing in his appearance or behaviour supports the tomcat stereotype, any more than his bearing reflects his royal moniker. Not that he answers to 'Charles' in particular; he comes running whatever name you call… Apparently there was some question of our King changing his name on his succession, on account of previous namesakes having dubious reputations, but he stayed with Charles, and so has our cat, Male Cat The First. 'Charles' is very much his name, even if he hasn't realised yet. Not Charlie.

What can I say about him, this little chap who nearly missed getting his own chapter? He's a cat with a ready purr which switches on at the slightest prompt: a kind word or stroke, a person joining him in his toilet. Lifted up, he's a warm, yielding bundle. I can carry him around, or stand hugging him, for as long as I like, and just get purred at. None of that uneasy wriggling many cats go in for, or the mighty twist-and-leap when nature kicks in and they just have to break free, rendering human arms powerless. None of my previous cats has been so easy to hold. When I was in therapy with Allan, I had a recurring dream that my cat was in danger, and I needed to carry her to safety, but she struggled in my arms even as I searched for a safe container. No Jungian worth his salt would be short of interpretations, especially for the version of the dream where I found a shop selling cat baskets at the same price that Allan charged for a session, and objected to the cost. But the instinctive struggling many cats go in for can be a problem, and I feel pleased that should Charles ever need removing from some dangerous situation, it will be easy. As well as being slightly built, he's light, though not as light as he was when he arrived back in February, or as small. He emerged from the carrier thin-tailed and flat-bodied, as though he'd been vacuum packed for travel, but in time he filled out into a more satisfying shape.

I can pick him up – another first - even if he's in the middle of a squabble with another cat, probably because his fights are just another kind of play, and he's always glad to interact with a human friend. His hunting is another matter, and one I respect too much to interrupt with demands for a cuddle. As previously stated, it took us a while to work out that he was the provider of the occasional corpses, but with the cooler weather the bodies became more frequent, two or three a day, and it was easier to see what was going on. While Luna and Poppy snoozed or pottered around the house and garden, Charles would spend whole mornings settled beside the fridge or cooker, eyes open, unmoving and silent, not looking up when I came over. Once I came down in the middle of the night to find him sliding a paw into a box of baking ingredients on the bottom shelf of the pantry. In the morning, Steve bravely rearranged the contents of the pantry and caught a glimpse of large brown rodent behind the freezer. I ran through the house and garden, even into the street, shouting 'Charles! Quick, a mouse', but when he turned up and was ushered into the pantry, he made straight for the cat flap. I kept him in the kitchen, urging him freezer-wards. Can cats look exasperated? It was entirely clear to Charles that the rodent had followed a route through the wall into the utility room and thence into the back garden, and he must have marvelled at my idiocy at keeping him inside. He sniffed around the cupboard at the back of the utility room where an old spin dryer hose had left holes in the wall, but half-heartedly, as if humouring me.

Charles's hunting and pouncing skills especially impressed me given his lack of binocular vision, but I've read since that cats use not principally their eyesight but their hearing, and their sense of smell, and minute vibrations in the air, to locate their pray. He always knows where the mouse is, and how it got there, and where it might go next. He sniffs the floor, tilts his head, crouches and listens, while I stand at a respectful distance and listen too, hearing nothing. I hate living things being killed, but I've come to rejoice in the efficiency, the beauty, of his expertise; and to admire his modesty, his workmanlike approach which is such a pleasure to watch in human craftsmen. Charles gets the job done with a smile. If he could whistle under his breath, he would. Except he wouldn't, because whistling would alert his prey.

'Workmanike', 'craftsmen' – these are gender-specific words, but I don't think Charles's hunting skill has anything to do with chromosomes. Katy and Fish were capable hunters too. Because they operated outside and brought the results inside, dead or alive, I had less opportunity to observe them, except with alarm. When I caught them at it I did my best to rescue the victim; there was no time to admire their technique, or to share the fervent anticipation, the silent concentration, of the hunter. The only time I've felt anything similar was on a walking safari in Zimbabwe years ago, where we were quietly following a black rhino which suddenly became aware of us and turned in our direction. The guide raised his riffle, and I felt a heady burst of adrenaline. I'd have hated to see a rare wild creature harmed, of course, but in that second I glimpsed the hormonal high of the hunt. Then the rhino turned away and the rifle was lowered, and we walked quietly on.

Back to Charles. He is out a lot in good weather, we know not what where, but probably quite some distance away. All three cats come at once when they hear us call, whatever name we use, so either he goes out of hearing or he's nearby but busy with something. He often looks busy, bustling in and out of rooms, on and off my lap with only a moment's rest in between. Presumably this activity is hunting related. He's always cheerful, unlike his sister who is given to soulfully loitering in the kitchen, meandering and mewling round our legs, like a poet with writer's block or (more likely) a bored moggy hoping for a treat. He likes to be busy, but in damp weather he can spend a whole day in his favourite sleeping place of the moment, currently the chaise longue in the front room, which is now known as the Charles Longue.

What else? He drinks a lot of water, but only from the cat fountain and only when it is switched on, or, if he must, out of the jug that is used to top up the bowl in the front room. I really hope this constant need to hydrate is not an early sign of kidney disease… He's a messy drinker, standing with one foot in the fountain and stirring vigorously as he laps, or sucking the water from his paw like a pet in an advert. He mostly eats biscuits, not soft food, and I hope that accounts for all the drinking.

Oh, and he is loyal to his sister, even though he winds her up at times. Any trouble with an intruder, and Luna's growl brings him to her side. In his thorough, patient way, he'll stake out the porch for hours after the strange cat has left and Luna has gone off for a nap. Hunting is his thing, but he seems to care about Luna's welfare too. When we had to take her to the vet, he ran down the drive alongside the yowling carrier and jumped up and down as we put it in the car, then waited in the front garden for her safe return. She ignored him, of course.

Anything else? I pause and think of nothing, so I reread what I've written, and it makes me smile. What a smashing little cat, and how strange that he tends to get overlooked. I don't think it's because he's male, I think it's because he's OK. A cheerful, sociable, busy, self-contained little cat with modest needs. A top class British Shorthair, and there is nothing better to say.

ANY QUESTIONS

'If you could ask your cat any question, what would it be?'

Interesting. I was filling in an online survey proffered by Facebook; another morsel of clickbait I had not managed to resist, even though it surely represented yet another means of collecting my data in order to sell me something, cat food or litter or remedies. The questions were dull until this last one, reminiscent of the final 'fun' round on Gardeners Question Time. If you could ask your cat any question (and get an intelligible answer, presumably), what would it be?

My first thought was that I'd ask the cat how she was. Did anything hurt; did she need anything. If only I could have asked Mia those questions. Did the painkillers help, would she still feel comfortable in her basket if I moved it somewhere less draughty, would she prefer me to call the emergency vet today, or wait to see if she felt better on Monday? These were the practical questions I agonised over, unable to sense her wishes. Most of the time we communicated so comprehensively with eye contact and touch that I felt no need to ask her anything, but she was a cat, and cats conceal their physical vulnerabilities to protect themselves, so perhaps she would have evaded verbal questions about her state of health.

But those days are past, and now I have three flesh and blood cats with no immediate medical needs. If I could ask each of them a question, what would it be?

Last month, I'd have asked the two new cats who was killing the mice, but that is no longer a mystery. I might instead request Charles to point out all the mouse-level entry points in the house so that we (well, Steve) could block them with wire wool and put an end to the infestations. Knowing Charles he would oblige, but I'd feel bad about putting him in that position because I'm sure his hunting role gives him much purpose and satisfaction. It would be like asking a prize employee to volunteer for redundancy... What else might I ask him? I'd be interested to hear what it feels like to track the movements of a rodent inside a wall, and to be told whether he ever tired of it. I can imagine his quizzical expression. 'Tired, when there's prey to stake out? I don't think so.'

Luna, then. I'd like to ask about her eating habits. What is the special attraction of the human meals I put on the table? Does she dislike cat food and feel constantly hungry, or does she crave a particular ingredient to balance some nutritional deficit? Or is her desire to annexe the contents of my plate, or to stand on the stove eating out of the frying pan, an expression of boredom? I can imagine posing the questions, but even if she were granted the power of speech, I don't think I'd get a straight answer. She does what she does and is not in the business of justifying it. 'What have you got against Poppy?' I might enquire, and she'd give her head a little shake and walk away. 'Luna! Do you love me?' A swish of that magnificent tail.

And Poppy? Back in January I'd have asked her whether she wanted us to get another cat, but she'd just have said she wanted Mia back. Come February, I might have enquired whether the two newbies had been a terrible mistake as far as she was concerned. Same in March. Same in April. Do you need any help, Poppy? Can you stand this situation? You're not thinking of leaving home? Trying to imagine these conversations makes me realise how clearly she communicates without human language. She likes her stroking done a certain way. She likes having her own supply of biscuits in the study, a privilege accorded during the days when going downstairs was dangerous, and which continued because it makes her happy and is very little trouble. I know how she feels about that special biscuit bowl because she purrs as she crunches. She likes the chair in the study positioned close to the bed so she can jump up more easily; I don't need to ask how she feels when somebody moves it, or (worse) sits on it, because her horrified stare, her circling of the room, her nudging at their knees, says it all. Poppy, come to think of it, is an excellent communicator, for matters within her grasp. 'Are you thinking of leaving home?' would have no meaning to her. She lives here, with us. 'Can you stand this situation?' likewise. This is the situation, and standing it is what she does.

Here is a question I'd like to ask every cat I've known: why, when you are meticulously clean in your habits, and you wipe a moistened paw over your face after ever meal and on many other occasions throughout the day, *do you never, ever, clean your eyes?*

A Life Told In Cats

They get gunky, weepy, develop crusts at the corners which can't be comfortable or hygienic, but you clean *round* them. Why? Surely that is a question that could be answered. I asked a vet once if she had any idea, and she said it was a mystery to her too. I wonder if the hypothetical speaking cat would offer a coherent explanation, or simply say, 'Obviously I don't clean my eyes. Nobody does'.

It is not easy to envisage a single Q and A that would yield anything new or useful. If dialogue in human language should ever become possible, I'd stick to offering information. 'We are having some building work in the utility room next week. Your food and water will be moved to the front room. The kitchen and patio will be full of clutter and noise and dust that will upset you, so please avoid the cat flap and use the porch window to get into the front garden. The work will be finished in eight days' time, then everything will go back where it was and be clean and tidy; also the radiator will work better, so your sleeping places will be warmer'.

That would be a useful bit of communication. Instead of which, the cats will observe with mounting alarm the removal of numerous objects from their proper places, the tension within and between the humans as they prepare, the early-morning onset of inexplicable sounds and vibrations which continue hour after hour, right through sleeping times and meal times and play times, followed by evenings and nights of nose-tickling chemical smells and dust and confusion.

I don't like having builders in the house myself, but at least I know that these guys are friendly and reliable, and that the work will come to an end quite soon. How must the vibrations of hammering and sawing affect Charles, alerted by a rustle or squeak two rooms away? How must Luna feel at human mealtimes, readying her muscles to jump on the table only to find that we, and the food, perhaps the table itself, are missing? Poppy, accustomed to living an old house with endless defects, takes disruption more easily; but coming downstairs of a morning, might she not be ambushed by the traumatised yowls and claws of the others? If only they could understand a few simple instructions. 'Poppy, wait until Luna's out of the way, she's upset by the builders'. 'Charles, I've put a blanket on the chair at the top of the garden in case the noise is too much'. 'Luna, poor Luna, come upstairs and sit on my knee until it's over. I'll stay here all day if you want me to. That's how much I want to make you happy. The building work is nothing to take personally.'

Some might accuse me of anthropomorphism even to be thinking of conversing with my cats, although I am trying to take account of the difference in species, as far as possible. It is hard enough reaching an understanding with human beings with a different first language. French is the only foreign tongue I know well, a European language sharing many roots with English, but there is a constant difficulty, translating between the two, in conveying the exact meaning, because each word and construct carries its own load of history and culture. How much more so between species. Cats may leave home if they are unhappy about some domestic detail or if they get a better offer elsewhere, but unless they have some means of communicating with each other that is opaque to humans, 'leaving home' is not a concept that a cat like Poppy, intimately attached to her home and her humans, could conceive of.

'Conceive of' – another anthropomorphism. They are everywhere. Was some of Taboo's skittish behaviour 'calculated'? Had she become 'over-identified' with her trauma, fearing that without it we would lose interest in caring for her? Did Jessica 'recognise' how charmed people were by her winsome tricks, and play to her audience? 'Calculate', 'identify', 'recognise'; some might say that the words are meaningless except for human beings with a spoken language. I would counter that if you spend time with a cat, get to know her really well, watch and listen to her behaviour, you find that so much of it is so similar to human reactions that you might as well use the same words to describe what is going on. Grief – that's a cat thing. I knew a cat who pined away and died six weeks after her sister was run over.

Excitement. Fear. Sheepishness, even. I would come into the bedroom sometimes to find Mia standing on the outside windowsill; this was long after she lost her youthful capacity to grip and balance. She would catch sight of my horrified face and slink back through the window and under the bed. Why should I not say that she 'knew' I'd be upset and 'wanted' to avoid facing me? The same when I came across her once in the middle of the road, sniffing the white line like a fluffy grey bloodhound. She actually jumped when she noticed me, and belted back up our drive. Why not use the words that match the experience rather than claiming that the higher animals operate entirely on 'instinct' without 'thought' or 'emotion'?

Claire Entwistle

Cat brains are smaller than ours both absolutely and relative to their body size, but they and we pretty much share the same brain structure and neurological systems; only 10% difference, apparently. Proportionally, cats devote more of their brains to the senses, smell and hearing and taste especially, while we are more visual creatures and have a larger area of brain reserved for – I don't know – sports trivia or the words of 1970's TV adverts. And composing music and studying astronomy and designing towns and writing computer code, of course, but not everyone performs these human-specific functions all or even most of the time.

Cats can appreciate music, anyway. Why not say 'appreciate'? A friend of ours, a professional soprano singer who came in to feed Taboo during one holiday and used our piano to practice while she was there, reported that Taboo loved the classics and would sit close and entranced as Carollyn sang the high notes. Opera was her favourite, but there were songs on the television or radio that she liked as well, especially a Christmas advert one year with high tingly bells, which made her sit up and purr every time.

I'm writing this mostly for people who love cats and enjoy watching them and commenting on what they find, but I also have in mind someone outside this category, an opposite sort of person (just as 'dog' is the opposite of 'cat'), who may by this point be muttering that most of what I'm saying is fanciful. I suspect that anyone who thinks that has never put in much time studying cats. Any animal you watch closely becomes more and more fascinating. I used to think that hamsters were dull until I looked after one for a month. An industrious little soul, he was, taking his regular exercise on the wheel, polishing his teeth on the bars, tidying his bedding and his toilet area, maintaining his space in tip-top order and from time to time having a bit of a change-around, transporting cotton wadding or peanut shells along the tubes of his 'glass home', as it was called. I can empathise with that; I am always moving things around at home. Daisy and I had hamsters when we were little, and I'd liked their small size and furriness, but didn't pay enough attention to enjoy all of this. A hamster, a mouse, a little bird, an insect – all marvels, in their own way, if you really look, and all resembling us more than they differ.

BACK TO THE PRESENT

Winter draws on, Valentine's day is far behind, and I am established in the three-cat regime. A strange and new phase of the Cycle: after three decades, I no longer have a cat.

Instead, I have three cats and the ever-present Mia, la mia Mia, my foot in the animal kingdom. True she has faded somewhat, her shadow around the house now the palest limestone grey. My head no longer turns towards her basket in the kitchen, sensing a movement, and I don't expect to see her waiting for me in the bathroom in the mornings, jumping into the bath and asking to have the tap on, and when at night the duvet shifts near my feet, I don't think she has joined us on the bed. But I think of her often, and her moving shadow in my mind, as strong and true as ever, dapples my thoughts.

Poppy has not become my cat. I didn't really think she would. I've always been fond of her, but after all those years of being Steve's cat, my contact limited for her own safety, that particular bond never developed. Now that Mia is not here to swipe Poppy's little head away from my stroking hand, or to growl if she gets too close, you might think she would jump at the chance of sitting on my knee, but she never has, even when invited, even when picked up and placed there. I don't think she ever really wanted to sit on my knee at all; most British Shorthairs don't. She was just following Mia, as usual.

However, Poppy has become my very good friend. My study is her chosen refuge in the daytime, my side of the bed her favourite place at night. She has finally, finally ditched her old ambivalence about being stroked, and lies or rolls close beside me, purring at top volume. I think she has forgotten Mia now but she vaguely recalls that time with me is something to relish, and she does relish it.

And we have Luna and Charles; our cats, but not mine. Because of Luna's difficulty settling with Poppy, it was months before we stopped wondering if rehoming would be the kindest option – a fresh start for her, with no existing pets. The question rose again, more pressingly: did the siblings need to stay together or could we, if we wanted to, keep just one? Charles, that would be of course, not Luna as I'd envisaged when I imagined a two-cat household with Poppy once more in the supporting role.

Perhaps any cat you are considering rehoming is not truly your cat, however much you like or love her. It was summer before we agreed that the arrangement was working well enough, and perhaps in that moment they became our cats.

Or maybe it was not quite like that. Maybe they were ours all along, right from that Valentine's Day text. When I thought, during those first tense weeks, of putting Luna into a carrier, with or without Charles, and sending her off to a new, cat-less home, hoping but not knowing that she would bond quickly with her new humans, it felt a terrible thing to do, even when hissy fits and flying fur were the order of the day.

Claire Entwistle

And now that this matter is settled, and Luna is staying, it is the bonding process that is the problem. Shorthairs are known for choosing one person as their own, and I'm pretty sure that Luna has chosen me, as I chose her before we even met. But the other side of exclusivity is jealousy, and that is getting in the way. In the evenings, as I sit on the chair I used to share with Mia, my feet up on the stool she made me buy and her blanket making the length of my legs cosier and easier to grip, I sometimes feel a delicate imprint on my calf as Luna makes her way towards my lap. Muscle memory sets off the deep relaxation of the old regime, then remembers that that is over and tenses up, but after a pause Luna moves forward to rub her head against my wrist, and purrs quietly, and her face takes on a softness that is very beautiful. She holds my gaze. Her tension begins to melt, mine with it.

Then she stiffens, leans over the arm of my chair to hiss, and I know Poppy is amongst us. Or maybe Charles. She yowls, and I know the intruder has come closer.

'Oh Luna,' I say, 'let it go, you're with me now.'

'Can't let it go,' she all but says. Honestly, I don't know why that question was raised about talking English to your cat; who needs spoken language when shrieks and gestures say so much. She yowls again and chases the intruder from the room, leaving me and my lap unoccupied and available, but she forgets to come back, or has lost the urge. I hear a thud as she lands on the kitchen table, and imagine her sniffing for crumbs. Cheese, or crisps, or whatever her heart desires at that moment more than my company.

Another, firmer paw on my knee, this time attached to a beige shoulder and a tilted head.

'Hello, Charles.'

He jumps up purring, curls with his back to me and goes straight to sleep. He likes to sit on a knee, mine or Steve's or a visitor's, but remains self-contained. Minutes later, something wakes him – perhaps a mouse's tail has flicked the inside of some distant wall – and he's off to check it out.

I smooth the blanket on my knees and look down to find myself staring into Poppy's astonished face.

'I know, Poppy, these are strange times. The government's just the same at the moment, people coming and going, taking fright, taking offence, getting distracted...'

I reach my hand down and she places her whole head in my palm and purrs as I scrunch her cheeks and ears. Soon she leaves too, heading for the cat flap and her nightly stroll, and I listen to the hasty clatter of claws on the kitchen floor, followed by an indignant moan, as she passes Luna. Brave Sir Poppy. Earlier this year we feared we would not have her for very long, she seemed so stiff and old and joyless, but now she seems years younger. I vaguely imagined an overlap of – ooh – a year or so. But that was Katy and Jessica. Shadow cats. Things can change. Poppy might outlive us all.

There has been a lot of purring in this cameo of life in a three-cat household, plenty of purring and stroking too. It's nice. But I don't have 'a cat', in the Mia or Fish sense, and none of them represents me in the way 'my cat' used to. Not that I don't identify with each of them in some ways, or aspire to some of their qualities. I'd like people to look at me in my old age as we look at Poppy, standing her ground for the first time in her life, and hear them murmur, 'So brave! Who'd have thought?' It would be delightful to discover that I was known, like Charles, for my good humour and dexterity, but perhaps our tilted heads would be a more obvious comparator. I'd love to be lithe as long-legged Luna, leaping into the rich red of the Japanese Maple, turning amber eyes to the camera, but I wouldn't want to be famous for my moodiness.

Everyone agrees that Luna is a lovely looking cat, but for me she doesn't approach perfection as closely as Mia did, or other British Blues that I've seen in real life or on photos. It may be time to accept that when she went, I lost that particular strain of beauty, perhaps forever. I'm in my early sixties writing this, living with two young cats who have just turned four; will there be time for another Blue in my life? I don't think so. And maybe that is the best thing. Maybe la mia Mia was a one-off, and what matters now is to move on to whatever the new phase is offering. Charles is such a sweetie, so full of unexpected talents. Poppy too, with her late-found courage.

And Luna! The very thought of her makes me smile, as the thought of Mia did and still does, on a good day. Mia had a song I used to sing to her, based around a simple riff, one that our little choir sings.

'Maria, mia bella, amore...' That's it. There's nothing to it really, but the notes soar with a kind of exaggerated joy, taking your heart with them. What could be easier than replacing 'Maria' with 'Mia'. My beauty, my love. It's accurate, but the hyperbole also makes me laugh. Your feelings and the expression of them can be so OTT, with and about a cat, and there's no comeback, at least from the cat herself, whatever that South London taxi driver may privately think. Your cat adores to be adored. As Allan said once, 'there is no end to the amount of love an animal will accept.' I forget what point he was making. It might have been important.

Luna is not mine yet, but I'm starting to think that she could be, especially now that she has a song of her own, or the beginnings of one. It goes to the tune of Baby Love.

> Luna love, my Luna love
> Brighter than the moon above
> I would sooner be with you
> Eating tuna, just us two
> Let me be your favourite hu-u-uman …

It needs some work, but it's possible that in spite of all the hissing and the nerviness and jealousy, all the stomping out of the room instead of staying with me to relax, she will become the new song of my life. La Luna Splende. But so too is Charles, mighty hunter, mighty purrer, named for our brand new King. Also Poppy, gallant Poppy, still with us. No longer one exquisite riff in my heart, but a three-part song made more interesting by a bit of discord here and there, a crunch of incompatible notes. This, with the haunting promise of harmonies to come, will be the next phase in the Cycle.

The Cat is dead. Long live the Cats.

Claire Entwistle

A Life Told In Cats

ABOUT THE AUTHOR

Claire is a life-long cat-lover who, despite the focus of this particular book, has been known to think about other things, including the elegant but demanding Edwardian house in Grange-over-Sands which she shares with her husband and three cats, and which will be the subject of her next book. Claire also works part-time as a psychotherapist, leads a small Natural Voice singing group and is co-Clerk of her local Quaker meeting.

Printed by Amazon Italia Logistica S.r.l.
Torrazza Piemonte (TO), Italy

40414322R00075